day trips® from
salt lake city

help us keep this guide up to date

We would love to hear from you concerning your experiences with this guide and how you feel it could be improved and kept up to date. Please send your comments and suggestions to:

editorial@GlobePequot.com

Thanks for your input, and happy travels!

day trips® series

day trips® from
salt lake city

first edition

getaway ideas for the local traveler

dale & michelle bartlett

gpp®
travel

Guilford, Connecticut

All the information in this guidebook is subject to change. We recommend that you call ahead to obtain current information before traveling.

ISBN 978-0-7627-5958-3

Printed in the United States of America
Distributed by National Book Network

contents

about the authors

First and foremost Dale and Michelle Bartlett are travelers in the truest sense of the word. Their love for adventure and desire to explore every corner have taken them throughout the world. They are passionate about doing more and paying less. Writing is their way of giving to others the ability to realize their own hopes and dreams of travels.

Dale and Michelle's travels have taken them throughout Europe, Central America, Mexico, and Canada and to nearly every state in the United States. They are best known for their family travels and their book, *Have Kids—Will Travel,* which teaches how any family, of any size, on any income can travel the world for just the cost of food and fun.

The Bartletts are highly sought speakers on the subject of traveling and they have shared their message throughout America. They have written articles for print as well as online magazines. They are also show hosts for The Women's Information Network, www.thewinonline.com, and have appeared on both radio and television advocating the importance of family travel.

When they are not discovering hidden treasures, the Bartletts make their home in the mountains of northern Utah. They have enjoyed rediscovering the immense diversity in their own "backyard" and finding the secrets of this great state. Learn more about the Bartletts at www.daytripsfromsaltlake.com.

acknowledgments

We recognize the many cities, tourism bureaus, hotels, and locals who have helped provide invaluable information as we wound our way through this amazing state.

Thanks to our incredible staff of researchers: Tawnee Wood, Michelle Lambert, Mary DeJong, Susan King, Jennifer Turner, Matt Lundgren, and especially Sasha Takis, who made sure the words we used were descriptive and fitting for such a beautiful part of the world.

To Brianne, Cameron, Devon, and Marissa and our friends, who were ignored for a time, who put up with our crazy travel schedules, and who support us in all we do—thank you.

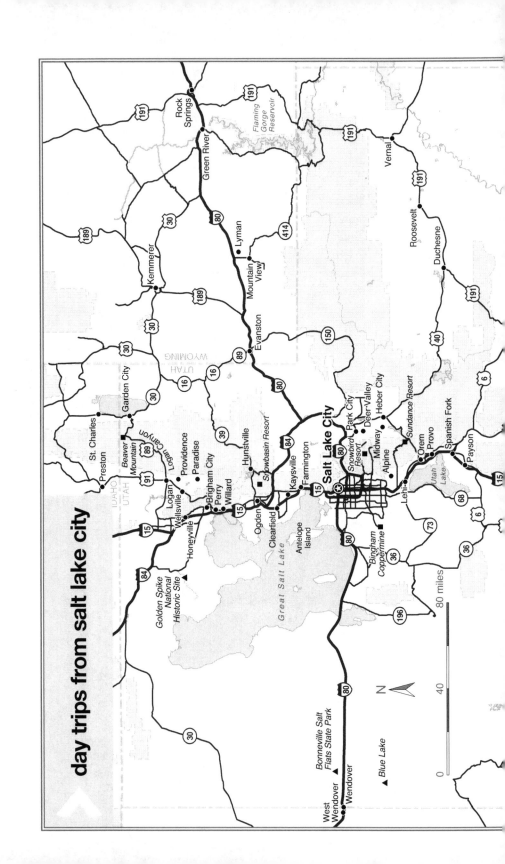

day trips from salt lake city

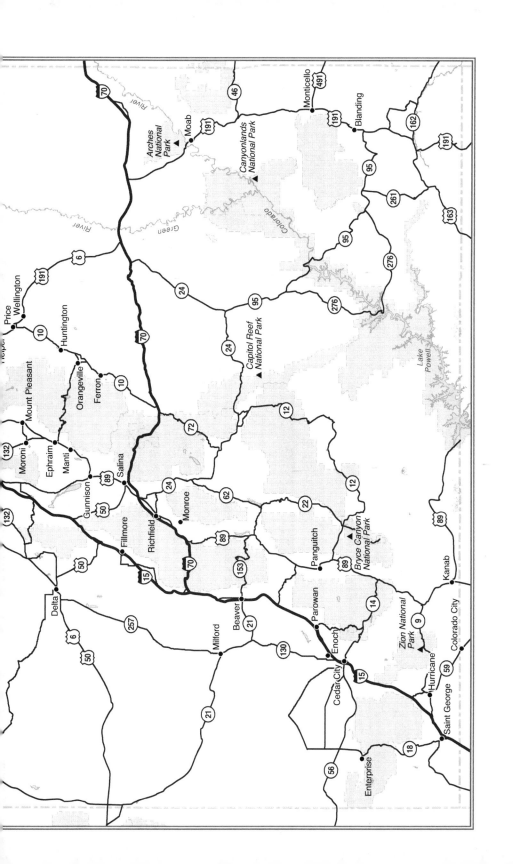

# introduction

Our family travels. We have traveled throughout the world and have seen many incredible places, people, and cultures. There is nothing like rounding a corner or cresting a hill in a place like Umbria, Italy, seeing for the first time a city set on a hill such as Assisi, and having an overwhelming feeling come over you . . . "Welcome home." As you explore the streets and talk with the locals, you get a sense you have been here before. This is the same feeling and sense we get when we explore our own backyard in Utah, and it's the same one we hope you will get as you explore *Day Trips from Salt Lake City*. Whether you are a Utah native, a newcomer, or a visitor to the state, "Welcome."

If you haven't explored, and we mean really explored, outside of Salt Lake City, you will never truly appreciate the vast diversity this part of the United States has to offer. Utah has been carved by nature as well as its varied cultures, and together they have sculpted this land into a vacationer's dream. *Day Trips from Salt Lake City* covers some of the most diverse territory anywhere, filled with national parks, steam engines, rockets, forests, and deserts, as well as little-known corners that count themselves among the variety of day trips you will find in this book.

Beginning as an inland sea, Utah was carved over time to create such diversity and beauty, much of it a rugged beauty, that it beckons millions to its borders every year. If you are an outdoor enthusiast, more is offered here than we could ever write about. If you are looking for wholesome destinations for family fun, this is the place. If you love little getaways where you can relax, we have added some of those, too.

Starting from the north in Cache Valley, where life seems less hurried, less bustling, yet full of culture and fine arts, we'll explore the Wild West as it was in the 1800s or a night at the theater or opera that will rival New York. In the south, where time nearly seems to stand still as you explore the many national parks like Bryce or Zion, often said to be the "most beautiful place on earth," we'll be given a view that has taken nearly two million years to form. East in Park City we'll show you where to find the calm, cool, and chic kind of fun that will make you feel like a star yourself. Film festivals, art shows, mining, and skiing give this once little mountain town a flavor all its own. Out west are the stark reminders of just how harsh this high desert can be. The Bonneville Salt Flats is one of the most unique natural features in Utah. Stretching over 30,000 acres, it has been the destination for visitors, commercial filmmakers, and high-speed enthusiasts."

Explore. Enjoy. In the words of St. Augustine, "The world is a book, and those who do not travel [even day trips] read only one page."

For more information on these day trips, visit www.daytripsfromsaltlake.com.

using this guide

Beginning north of Salt Lake City and following the compass clockwise, this guide will help organize each day trip starting from the closest to Salt Lake to the farthest destination for that point on the compass. All attempts have been made to keep the points of reference along major highways and byways, with a few deviations so as to separate best the neighboring destinations.

In each day trip there are several options, and for many there is more than a day's worth of activities and places to eat. We have included family activities, places for independent explorers, and romantic getaways. We have tried to provide a wide range of options for just about any lifestyle and curiosity.

Because of the uniqueness of the area, we have taken some liberties beyond the typical "day trip." Though all the trips listed can be done from Salt Lake City in a day, some may be more enjoyable if a night stay is included. We have therefore added a few more than the usual accommodations suggestions for this type of book.

Listings under Where to Eat, Where to Stay, and Where to Shop are listed in alphabetical order. Listings under Where to Go are sometimes ordered by the foremost attractions on the trip.

All distances and travel times are provided as they relate to downtown Salt Lake City crossroads of I-15 and I-80. It doesn't take long to get out of the hustle and bustle and begin your adventure away from the traffic and confusion of the city.

hours of operation, prices, credit cards

Included in this guide are details on business hours, pricing, and payment options as available at the time of publication. Please use the provided websites and phone numbers to call ahead to see if there have been any changes. Also ask if they are running any pricing specials not known at the time of publication.

pricing key

where to eat

The price code reflects the average cost of dinner entrees for 2, not including drinks, wine, appetizers, desserts, tax, or tip. Keep in mind that breakfast and lunch cost much less but may not be available at all restaurants listed.

$ Less than $30

$$ $30 to $50

$$$ More than $50

If you find yourself staying overnight, stay in a hotel that offers a free breakfast; look for local vendors for lunch and have more money in your pocket for an incredible dinner.

where to stay

Even though this book is designed for day trips, there are times when you will fall in love with an area and want to stay a little longer and explore a little more. The pricing codes below are designed to reflect the average cost of a double-occupancy room during peak pricing times. These prices do not include taxes or other fees that may be included in your final bill. They also do not include any discounts such as AAA, senior, military, or corporate rates.

$ Less than $100

$$ $100 to $150

$$$ $150 to $200

$$$$ More than $200

A tip for all accommodations: Hotels that cater to the business traveler are much less expensive on the weekend. Likewise, places that cater to the weekend traveler, like a B&B, are traditionally less busy during the week and provide better pricing during this time.

driving tips

The diversity of Utah's landscape provides both beauty and the occasional unexpected delay due to construction, landslides, heavy snow (even early fall and late spring), and rock-slides as you make your way through beautiful but sometimes remote areas of the state. It is said that there are two seasons for Utah road conditions—construction and winter. The easiest way to see Utah is by car; however, Utah recently added a commuter rail system that travels north to Ogden from Salt Lake City and in the future will be heading south to Provo. This may be an option for some of the day trips heading in those directions. Check schedules and stops as they are limited and you may find your final destination quite a walk from the station.

The road conditions vary based on the time of year and area you are traveling: dry and hot in the summer, cold and snowpacked in the winter (and there are times when you experience both in the same day). Make sure you take the precautions needed and have the proper equipment for the day trip.

Utah cities and towns are nearly always laid out in a north/south/east/west grid. There are only a few exceptions. When you get used to using the system, you will be able to find any address easily using the coordinates of the address. (For example, if the address is 610 S. 300 East, from Center and Main it is located just over 6 blocks south and 3 blocks east.)

highway designations

All Interstates are indicated with an "I."

US highways are usually 2- and sometimes 4-lane undivided roads. They are indicated with the standard US shield, with the highway number inside, or just "US" as in US 89.

State routes are either indicated by an oval with the route number in them or with either an "SR" or the state prefix "UT," as in SR 30 or UT 30.

highway quirks

Many of the US and state routes are often known by their local street names. For example, US 91 and US 89 combine together in Logan and are known as Main Street to the locals and the street signs. Through Salt Lake and Utah Counties, US 89 is known as State Street.

travel tips

There are 2 area codes in Utah. For all calls made to Salt Lake, Davis, Weber, and Utah Counties, use 801. For all outlying counties use 435. If you are using a cell phone, check with your provider. Many are now requiring the full 10-digit number to place a call, so remember where you are and the area code needed.

Sales tax is charged statewide. You will pay tax on all items including food purchased at the grocery. Expect to pay additional county and city taxes as well as premium hotel occupancy tax and fees.

where to get more information

Day Trips from Salt Lake City attempts to cover a variety of bases and interests, but those looking for additional material can contact the following agencies by phone, mail, or the web. Regarding the latter, be aware when checking various destinations that online reviews may vary based on personal preference. Be conscious of ratings such as AAA and Better

Business Bureau and call the place directly, as each area, city, and even attraction may have its own tourism board. In addition to these resources (keep in mind we have listed visitor centers, when available, with each of the day trips also to be used as a reference), a few other helpful sources include:

Day Trips from Salt Lake website
www.daytripsfromsaltlake.com

UTA Trax & FrontRunner
In Salt Lake City RIDE-UTA (743-3882)
In state (888) RIDE-UTA (888-743-3882)
www.rideuta.com (click on the Route Schedules tab on the right)

Utah
www.utah.com

Utah Bed & Breakfast Guide
www.utahbedandbreakfast.net

Utah State Historical Society
300 S. Rio Grande St.
Salt Lake City, Utah 84101
(801) 533-3500
www.history.utah.gov

Utah state and national parks
www.utah.com/nationalparks
www.utah.com/stateparks

Utah Office of Tourism
(801) 538-1900 or (800) 200-1160
www.travel.utah.gov

Utah Department of Parks and Recreation
1594 W. North Temple St., Suite 116
Salt Lake City, Utah 84116
(801) 538-7220 or (877) UT-PARKS
parkscomment@utah.gov
www.stateparks.utah.gov

north

day trip 01

north

wickedly fun, wet or dry:
farmington, kaysville

A short drive north of Salt Lake City, you will find amusement aplenty and beauty abound. Once small, quiet farming communities, Farmington and Kaysville have retained their slower-paced feel yet added a hint of fun and excitement to the air. From the largest amusement parks in the state to the local theatrical arts programs, Farmington has something for everyone. On the outskirts of Kaysville you will rediscover nature and see how the use of sustainable principles can not only reduce the impact on land and other resources but can provide an oasis for the soul in the midst of an ever-increasingly busy world and hectic life. Additionally prepare yourself to get wet in Kaysville at Cherry Hill Water Park and attractions. Miniature golf, batting cages, and rock climbing are among the myriad activities enjoyed.

What is incredible about this area is the feeling of seclusion from the city while being less than an hour away. You can get lost for a day, whether on a roller coaster or in the serene setting of a garden.

farmington

Known as the "City of Roses," the city of Farmington was settled in the mid 1850s as the county seat. This farming community has grown and developed yet has been able to maintain a small-town feel. Small local restaurants and shops are nestled throughout and are overlooked by the majestic mountains above. Hiking, biking, and other outdoor activities are plentiful. Farmington also has a rich community theater. You can check out

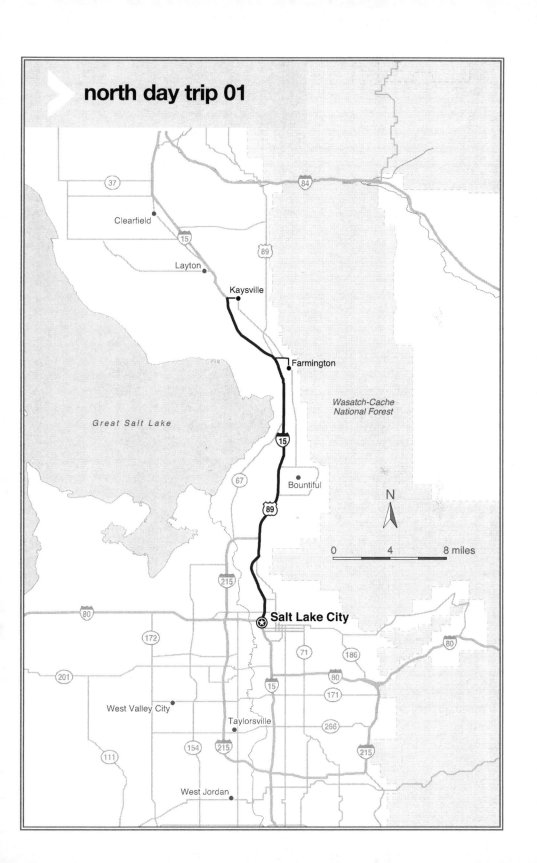

north day trip 01

what is playing by visiting the **Farmington Arts Blog** (www.farmingtonarts.blogspot.com). Farmington continues to grow, adding additional shopping and entertainment as they build the new Station Park Shopping Center in coming years. This center will have the look and feel of the Gateway Center in Salt Lake City, which will give Farmington a new, bigger, and sophisticated feel.

getting there

Take I-15 north from Salt Lake City about 17 miles. Take the Lagoon Drive/Farmington exit 322 and follow the signs, screams, and fun.

Farmington can also be accessed using the **UTA FrontRunner** train. See schedule for times and details; www.rideuta.com.

where to go

Lagoon Amusement and Water Park. 375 Lagoon Dr.; (801) 451-8000; www.lagoon park.com. Lagoon has a vast array of rides and activities within the boundaries of the park. It is fun-filled and has many features for the young and the old as well as the easy rider or the high-adventure thrill seeker. The attractions within the park will keep you entertained and captivated for an entire day of laughter and memorable activities. From roller coasters to sky rides, the park will be sure to please.

One of the most thrilling rides that is included with the purchase of a day pass is called **The Rocket.** This ride shoots you an amazing 200 feet in the air in less than 3 seconds! One of the most popular rides within the park is the **Lagoon "white" Roller Coaster,** which is over 80 years old. This piece of history remains one of the last remaining wooden roller coasters between Denver and the West Coast. Sit back and hold on tight as you experience the newest ride, **Wicked.** You won't know why you'll want to ride it again and again, just know you will. The thrill and speed of this ride will make you wonder when it is over, "What just happened?"

Kiddieland is an area catering specifically to Lagoon's younger guests. This section has many rides that are able to accommodate parents sitting next to their youngsters, allowing parents to enjoy the giggles of their little ones. A priceless experience!

To the east of the park, you can take a trip into the past by entering **Pioneer Village.** This Wild West section transports you back in time over 100 years. The quaint little village has been reconstructed to replicate a frontier community, with buildings that were donated by the Utah Sons of the Pioneers. Here you are able to visit authentic homes, buildings, and mercantile stores, all filled with wonderful artifacts from the past. Relax as you take an easy stroll on rustic wooden sidewalks, eating the creamiest of ice cream, or get an old-time photo of yourself dressed in your favorite historical attire. Within Pioneer Village guests can enjoy the splash on **Rattle Snake Rapids.** This ⅓-mile river-raft ride transports you swiftly through white-water rapids and swells. Just try to stay dry as you pass through a cave with a waterfall! Umbrellas anyone?

Lagoon-A-Beach surf and slide is located in the center of the amusement park. Six acres of waterslides will have you screaming, a lazy river will help you relax, and a center island just for little kids will guarantee all members of your family will stay cool during those hot summer days.

Another unique attraction that has continually been a crowd pleaser is the high-quality family entertainment and musical shows. Talented performers will put on a show that will have you tapping your feet and singing along to your favorite songs from both the past and the present.

The park opens the last week in May and runs daily through the end of Aug, operating 11 a.m. to 11 p.m., with a separate weekend-only schedule in Sept. A special **Fright-mares!** season, filled with ghoulish attractions, spook alleys, and lots of candy runs exclusively on weekends (Fri from 5 to 10 p.m., Sat and Sun from 11 a.m. to 10 p.m.) from the end of Sept through the end of Oct.

where to eat

There is a variety of food choices in the park. The park also allows visitors to bring their own food and picnic items inside.

Arby's. Located in the park, with a variety of roast beef and chicken sandwiches. The popcorn chicken is a hit with kids. $

Burger Express. Located in the park, with a choice of burgers, chicken, and fries. Kids' meals and souvenir drinks are available. $

Francisco's Mexican Grill. 7 E. State St.; (801) 451-0383. Open Mon through Sat and closed on Sun. Serving traditional Mexican meals at an incredible value for breakfast, lunch, and dinner, Francisco's is a local and visitor's favorite. The service has that personal touch you expect from a small restaurant. They are usually quite busy, so get there early or be prepared for a bit of a wait (though it is well worth that wait). $

Park Subway. A selection of 6-inch and foot-long sandwiches for just about every taste, including a Veggie Delight. $

where to stay

Lagoon RV Park and Campground. 375 Lagoon Dr., just south of the Lagoon Amusement Park; (800) 748-5246; www.lagoonpark.com. This is an easy and convenient place to stay while visiting Lagoon, with variable rates depending on the amenities desired. Water, electricity, and sewer are available for the RV camper, as well as tent sites for the rustic camper. The campground is open during Lagoon's running season, weather permitting. $

kaysville

As you drive towards Kaysville, notice that the city is surrounded by the beautiful Rocky Mountains to the east and the Great Salt Lake to the west. Kaysville was settled in 1850 and is now known for its quiet bedroom-type community, offering a rural atmosphere with peace and tranquility. Kaysville's downtown was renovated in the 1980s, combining its historic charm with a transformed economic energy. Visit the art gallery or spend a day on the golf course. Kaysville provides that welcome-home feeling.

where to go

Utah Botanical Center. 725 S. 50 West; (801) 593-8969; www.utahbotanicalcenter.org. The educational opportunities at the Botanical Center are innovative and varied. There are many workshops and children's events that run throughout the year. All activities and demonstrations are eco-friendly and use only recycled products. Spring and fall offer special family nights with fun, hands-on activities. Summer months allow visitors to enjoy the harvest of fresh, locally grown fruits and vegetables at the Farmers Market. Visitors are invited to visit the beautiful Butterfly Garden, the Wildflower Meadow, and the Urban Forest, as well as walk along the trails to The Ponds. Don't forget to drop by the Children's Discovery House to make your trip complete. The activities are endless, from teaching children to cook using only solar power, to learning how to make wizardly potions. Bugs, worms, and icky things will become a source of intrigue as children enjoy hands-on experiments. The love of exploration will be implanted in your little ones' minds for years to come. Summer day camps are also available and are located at the Utah House, 920 S. 50 West; (801) 544-3089.

Cherry Hill Water Park. 1325 S. Main St.; (801) 451-5379: www.cherry-hill.com. If you are looking for a full day of water fun, this is the place to go. Pirates Cove has a 40-foot pirate ship that makes everyone feel as if they were on the Caribbean protecting their treasure. The simulated ocean sounds and cannon blasts will have all crew members rallying around their captain. If a pirate's life isn't quite for you, head to the Grant's Gulch Lazy River. Relax on a tube and enjoy the ease of floating around as the day fades about you.

Looking for high adventure? Well then, try **Canyon River Run.** The many caverns and sudden drops and turns will keep the thrill alive throughout the entire ride. If you're feeling really daring, try the Double Dragons waterslide and travel at high speeds with fog and lightning in the tunnels! When it is time to put the sunscreen away, go ahead and try the 18-hole miniature golf course or the batting cages. Both activities will bring out smiles and maybe even a little friendly competition—but hey, who really keeps score?

Boondocks. 525 S. Deseret Dr.; (801) 660-6800; www.boondocksfuncenter.com. If you are looking for fun place to spend some time with your family, this can be constant excitement for the entire day or just a few hours. Because they offer so many activities, it is truly hard to just stay a few hours. We spent hours just playing in the 2-story laser tag arena. If it wasn't for working up such a good sweat, we would probably still be there! Boondocks provides a variety of entertainment options that will appeal to both young and old. They also offer 20 lanes of bowling, a video and redemption arcade and prize center, a soft play area for children, and the Back Porch Grill Restaurant, which serves hamburgers, salads, sandwiches, and desserts. The outdoor activities include a bumper boat pond, a 5-stall batting cage, 2 elaborate 18-hole miniature golf courses, and 2 go-cart racetracks. Now go win that game!

where to shop

Bun Basket N Bakery. (801) 593-9756. If you are hoping for a mouthwatering lunch or snack, you have to see what the Bun Basket n Bakery has in the oven for you. (The bread-sticks are the perfect end to a perfect day of shopping.)

Canyon Gallery, www.canyongallery.net, will make you feel right at home as you browse the original artwork, books, gifts, porcelains, bronzes, and much, much more.

Hidden Closet, (801) 444-9207, has the most fabulous style in women's clothing and accessories. You won't want to leave empty handed.

Rock Loft. 251 S. Mountain Rd.; (801) 544-3766. This is a fun little shopping area that encompasses some great shops and a bakery. Here's one fun place in the Rock Loft:

   Secret Haven is an eclectic uptown home decor and furniture store. They also sell jewelry, purses, and many exquisite homemade gifts. This is one of the best boutiques this side of the Rockies. Their designers and buyers are very talented. It's one of those hidden treasures you find only once in a while.

where to eat

Cherry Hill Pie Pantry. 1247 S. Main St.; (801) 451-7437. Of course the highlight of this shop is the selection of homemade fruit pies—especially cherry—but they serve a variety of other items: ice cream, cookies, wraps, sandwiches, etc. Come in for an afternoon of downright good food. $

Joanie's Restaurant. 286 N. 400 West; (801) 593-0374. If you're craving a home-cooked breakfast to start your day, Joanie's is the place to get it. You won't go away hungry! $

day trip 02

north

trains, planes & dinosaurs:
clearfield, ogden

Clearfield and Ogden are a relatively short distance from one another, but they present a tale of two cities with very different pasts whose futures today are tied together. Take a mix of farming, manufacturing, and local business, throw in a heavy dose of military might and even a Navy Depot (where's the water, guys?), and you have the makings for a very interesting day trip. The colorful and rich rail past has also played a significant role in this area. Today as you drive through these cities you come in contact with much of what makes up this region of the Salt Lake Basin and see how it tries to hold onto its past while it "soars" into the future. From the daily jet engines of Hill Air Force base reaching high in the sky to the downtown streets of Ogden (25th Street), you begin to sense how past and present have come together. Just think—there was a day when Al Capone walked out of the train station in Ogden and commented that this place was too wild a town for him! Today Al would find a more tourist-friendly Ogden, but with a preserved architectural past that gives the city a charm all its own.

clearfield

This small but progressive city is situated between the beautiful Great Salt Lake on the west and Hill Air Force Base on the east. Throughout the years Clearfield was known as a quiet and peaceful farming community, but in 1940 construction of Hill Air Force Base began and eventually the facility ran along the town's eastern border. Clearfield is home to technology,

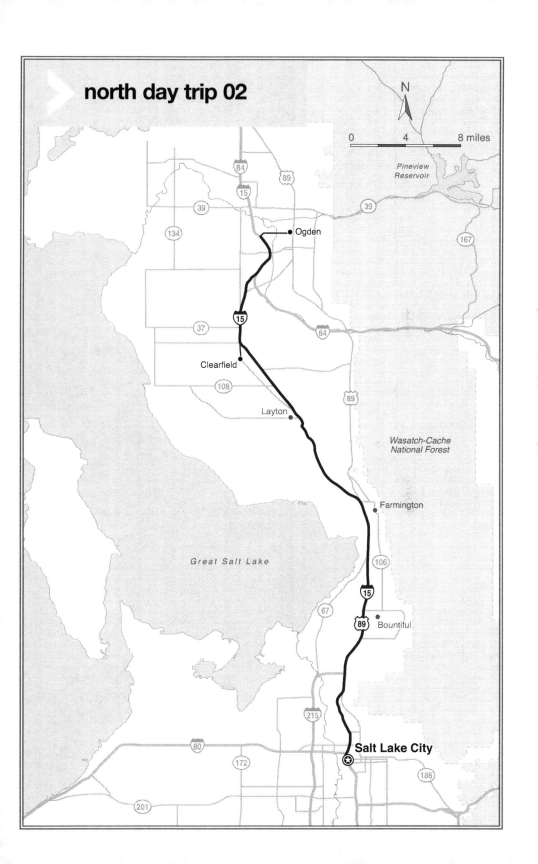

north day trip 02

N

0   4   8 miles

Pineview
Reservoir

84
89
15

39   39

134   167

● Ogden

15

37   84

Clearfield ●

108

89

Layton ●

Wasatch-Cache
National Forest

Farmington ●

Great Salt Lake

106

15

67

89   ● Bountiful

215

80

172

★ **Salt Lake City**

201   186

education, commerce, and several nationally known companies. Because of the quality of life in this community as well as access to several golf courses, ski resorts, nature trails, and wildlife, Clearfield is one of the fastest growing cities in the nation. Clearfield is also known as "A Great Place to Live, Work, and Play!"

getting there

Travel north from Salt Lake City 29 miles and take exit 335. Turn right to Hill Air Force Base or left to Main Street, then left on Main Street for Clearfield City. To go to the Aerospace Museum, go 3 miles further north on I-15 to exit 338 and turn right. You can't miss it.

where to go

Hill Aerospace Museum. Take the Roy exit 338; 75th ABW/MU, 7961 Wardleigh Rd., Building 1955; Hill Air Force Base; (801) 777-6868 or (801) 777-6818; www.hill.af.mil/library. The museum is located on the northwest corner of Hill Air Force Base, about 5 miles south of Ogden.

Did you ever wonder when you were a kid what it would be like to soar through the skies on a clear, crisp morning? The Hill Aerospace Museum will make you feel almost as though you were flying these planes, as you are allowed to sit in and pretend to "fly" some of the most amazing aircraft ever made. There are more than 90 military aircraft, missiles, and vehicles on the grounds and inside the 2 galleries.

There is also a selection of military vehicles, uniforms, and aerospace ground equipment and thousands of other historical artifacts. They have an array of educational information that can teach visitors about the history, function, and mission of the US Air Force and the importance of Hill Air Force Base in our nation's defense.

Open 7 days a week from 9 a.m. to 4:30 p.m. Admission is free but monetary donations are gratefully accepted. There are 3 days of the year that they actually close: New Year's Day, Thanksgiving Day, and Christmas Day. Let's see how high you can fly—just imagine!

ogden

Ogden will take you to myriad places as you explore, from the serenity and playfulness of the mountains to the eclectic vibe of the famously charming Historic 25th Street. You won't find any skyscrapers other than mountain peaks: Ben Lomond Peak, Strawberry Peak, and Mt. Ogden.

Ogden was the home to the Great Salt Lake Fremont Indians. After the Fremonts came the Northern Shoshone and Goshute tribes. With the building of Fort Buenaventura by European settlers and the following shortly thereafter of the transcontinental railroad, Ogden became better known. In March of 2002 *Sunset* magazine named Ogden as the city with the "best access to the outdoors." *Sunset* talked extensively about Ogden's hiking and biking trails and the awesome views from the mountaintops.

getting there

Travel north on I-15 about 35 miles to exit 342 (24th Street). Take a right on Pennsylvania Avenue and remain right onto 24th Street. Stay on 24th Street (you'll pass Fort Buenaventura Park) until you reach Washington Avenue. Turn right and you are downtown Ogden.

Note: Ogden is one of the Utah towns that threw away the traditional street numbering scheme everyone else in Utah uses. Instead they opted for a more patriotic theme. If you are familiar with the American presidents, then getting around shouldn't be a problem. Ogden is bordered to the north by North Ogden City, to the south by South Ogden City, to the west by West Haven, and to the east by the Wasatch Mountain Range. The streets in Ogden from west to east are named after the American presidents, starting with one of the main roads, Washington Boulevard on the west side of town, and ending with Buchanan Avenue on the east side of town. Roads from north to south are numbered starting with 1st Street. Downtown Ogden is located between about 20th Street and 30th Street from north to south and from Wall Avenue to Monroe Avenue from west to east.

where to go

Ogden Nature Center. Follow 1-15 north from Salt Lake then take exit 344 and head east 1.5 miles; 966 W. 12th St.; (801) 621-7595; www.ogdennaturecenter.org. If you are searching for a little bit of nature amongst the crowd and concrete you'll find many wonderful adventures here. Located in the heart of Ogden, this 152-acre nature preserve and education center boasts several ponds, trails (including the Birdhouse and Habitat trails) for viewing wildlife, and even a tree house. Visitors can choose from a wide variety of workshops and classes that will appeal to all ages, including subjects such as wildlife in Utah, outdoor recreation, conservation, sustainability, birding, photography, and art. There are summer camps, winter activities, and more. Be sure to bring a picnic. Open Mon to Fri 9 a.m. to 5 p.m. and Sat 9 a.m. to 4 p.m.

Ogden/Weber Convention and Visitors Bureau. 2438 Washington Blvd.; (801) 778-6250 or (866) 867-8824; www.ogden.travel. If you go to the website, there is free *Guidebook for Ogden* that you can download, which is a great way to find all the hidden treasures Ogden has to offer. You can also pop in to the Visitors Bureau, where they are more than happy to answer any of your questions (and depending on what you are doing they may just want to tag along). Whatever adventure you are hoping for, you will not be disappointed with Ogden.

Peery's Egyptian Theater. 2415 Washington Blvd.; (801) 689-8700; www.peerysegyptiantheater.com. If you want to experience some entertainment the whole family can enjoy, you need to visit Peery's Egyptian Theater. It will feel like you are back in the 1920s, as this historical movie palace has been fully restored to its former glory and offers many exciting and high-end live performances as well as cinema. Presentations include ballet, comedy, Celtic, country, dance, drama, music, film, holiday, classic, international, and more. As a part of the Ogden Eccles Conference Center, Peery's Egyptian Theater is the cornerstone of the revitalization for the downtown area. They are committed to keeping the arts alive and shining brightly—yes, bright as stars!

Fort Buenaventura. 2550 A Ave.; (801) 399-8099; www.co.weber.ut.us/parks/fortb. Watch out, because you may feel like you've stepped back in time . . . but don't worry, there are no Indians looking to ambush you. Built in 1845 by fur trapper and horse trader Miles Goodyear and his Ute Indian wife, Fort Buenaventura has since been reconstructed on the original site after much historical and archaeological research. Located on an 84-acre river tract of land near Weber River, many mountain men gathered here annually to trade with the Indian tribes (the legendary rendezvous), trap the rivers for beaver, and live off the land. While visiting you can enjoy camping, picnic areas, canoeing, touring the fort, shopping at the Trading Post, and watching reenactments of the famous rendezvous on special occasions.

Experience the **Spring Rendezvous** held on Easter weekend each year, which marks the opening of their season. Enjoy the **Music Festival,** which is 3 full days of a variety of music, food, and fun the first of June. During the month of July the fort offers free outdoor movies with live entertainment 2 hours before sunset. You can take a canoe for a ride, listen to the music, tour the fort, and then relax with your lawn chair or blanket as you watch the movie under big, beautiful stars. **Pioneer Skills and Crafts Day Fair** is usually held on July 24. Like the Spring Rendezvous, the **Labor Day Rendezvous** will have a fur trade, trader's row, primitive camping, shooting contests, canoe races, and much more during the first part of Sept. The **Turkey Shoot** is held the weekend before Thanksgiving, your lucky chance to dust off the ol' smoke pole and win yourself some grub. Rifle contests fill the morning with black powder shotguns. Come early and shoot often (is the advice that they give at Fort Buenaventura).

Ogden's George S. Eccles Dinosaur Park. 1544 Park Blvd.; (801) 778-6250; www.dinosaur park.org. If you dare, take a look around the Dinosaur Park. You will discover multiple things—some you'll want to and some you won't! Keep a look out for Zane the Dino Brain, who will explain the why paleontology is the "Science of Cool." The Dinosaur Park gives you an extreme, larger-than-life look at the life and times of the fiery dinosaur world. As you walk around the park, you will be up close and personal with the dinosaurs, as if you can feel them moving right behind you (and actually many times they are). As Zane puts it, "These bad boys look REAL—sometimes TOO real." There is a working paleontology lab, hands-on exhibits, and over 8 acres of life-sized dinosaurs in an outdoor park setting. Children will enjoy digging for fossils, running amongst the beasts, and getting the wiggles out on the playground. Call for hours as they vary by season.

Treehouse Children's Museum. 347 E. 22nd St.; (801) 394-9663; www.treehouse museum.org. The Treehouse Museum is known for being a "magical place where children and families step into a story." The Museum was founded in 1992 by a group of parents, educators, and business leaders who wanted to create a place for families. It has also been a great resource for area schools that have had the privilege of enjoying the exhibits, performances, and other offerings. Exhibits in the imaginative play area are: The Treehouse, The Baby Place, Days of the Knights, Pick up a Stick and Play Music Room, and One World Village. Hands-on literacy exhibits are: Great American Map, Oval Office, Dinosaur Discovery and Color Canyon, The One Room School, Mapping Utah, The Art Garden, Castle Theatre, and Millennium Tales. Have your boys ever wanted to be a knight for the day? If so, this is their opportunity to finally be knighted. Open Mon 10 a.m. to 4 p.m., Tues to Thurs and Sat 10 a.m. to 6 p.m., and Fri 10 a.m. to 8:30 p.m.

East Canyon Resort and Reservoir. East Canyon Reservoir is in East Canyon between I-80 and I-84. To access this beautiful destination you can take UT 66 from Morgan, exit 103 off I-84. Other routes: from the south, UT 65, exit 134 off I-80 in Parley's Canyon, or the north, exit 115 off I-84 in Henefer. UT 66 follows the north shore of the reservoir, and UT 65 follows the east shore. East Canyon State Park; 5535 S. US 66, Morgan; (801) 829-6866; www.utah.com/stateparks/east_canyon.htm. This popular reservoir drains the Snyderville Basin area, including Park West Ski Resort, and offers many recreational adventures year-round. There are 680 acres to enjoy with boating, year-round fishing, camping, swimming, and much more. Come and be delighted as you relish the heavenly surroundings of this beautiful edifice that is nestled in the mountains of Salt Lake.

Ogden Union Station Foundation. 2501 Wall Ave.; (801) 393-9886; www.theunion station.org. With the railroad history in Ogden, Union Station stands as a monument. The transcontinental railroad brought many cultural and economic changes to the area. Union Station hosts a multitude of museums and galleries: the **John M. Browning Firearms Museum,** the **Browning Kimball Car Museum,** the **Natural History Museum,** and the **Utah State Railroad Museum/Eccles Rail Center** (which displays 2 of the largest locomotives ever manufactured anywhere). You can enjoy lunch or dinner at the **Union Grill,** or shopping at **Gifts at the Station** or **Zephyr Station** (model railroad shop). "All aboard" for many fun adventures in the heart of Ogden!

The Junction. 2351 Kiesel Ave. At the heart of central plaza, The Junction is a 20-acre entertainment, residential, office, and retail center, which acts as a gathering place and event venue for the populace. Anchored by a **Megaplex 13** movie theater and the Salomon Center, there is much to see and do here.

The Salomon Center. 2351 Kiesel Ave.; (801) 399-4653; www.salomoncenter.com. The center, which has entertainment and extreme adventures, offers multiple activities, including bowling, glow in the dark golf, electric bumper cars, billiards, arcade, indoor surfing (don't forget your swimsuit), a 55-foot climbing wall, and iFLY—an indoor wind tunnel for skydiving. iFLY is located 2261 Kiesel Ave., Suite 200; (801) 528-5348; www.iflyutah.com. If you want a truly exhilarating and heart-pounding adventure, you need to sign up for just a few minutes of "fly time." This truly gave us an adrenaline rush just from watching others. It's not for the faint of heart!

where to shop

Artist & Heirlooms. 115 Historic 25th St.; (801) 699-0606; www.artistsandheirlooms.com. This gallery features fine artwork, antiques, collectibles, jewelry, and home decor. On the first Fri of each month from 6 to 9 p.m., you can meet the artists and listen to live music as you enjoy light refreshments. Open Mon through Sat 11 a.m. to 6 p.m.

Historic 25th Street. 175 Historic 25th St.; (801) 392-7573; www.historic25.com/ogden-25th-street. 25th Street is the center of Ogden's Historic District. This beautiful area is home to some of the most culturally diverse establishments. You can stroll down the street and talk with the artists at local galleries, meander around a few boutiques, check out a museum, or stop to enjoy some great cuisine. There are more places than you can count, so here are just a few:

Indigo Sage. 195 Historic 25th St., Suite 1; (801) 621-7243; www.indigosagegallery.com. Fun and sassy, elegant and stylish, or rustic and simple—you have found the place for it all. Although they sell home furnishings and decor, they also have small gift items spanning eclectic, European, and mountain luxury. You will be enchanted and inspired as you stroll around this unique store. Open Mon through Sat 10 a.m. to 6 p.m.

Little Cherry Blossoms. 184 Historic 25th St.; (801) 334-0184; www.littlecherryblossoms .com. The relaxing and kid-friendly atmosphere at this store makes it a pleasure to shop. You will find unique clothing for your children or next baby gift. They also offer creative and educational toys for your children to investigate.

Making Scents. 151 25th St.; (801) 866-0303; www.mkngscnts.com. Making Scents is a wonderful secret. They offer personal bath and body products where you choose the product and fragrance, making it your own personal creation. Open Mon through Sat 10 a.m. to 6 p.m.

Rainbow Gardens. 1875 Valley Dr.; (801) 392-1777; www.rainbowgardens.com. Located at the mouth of scenic Ogden Canyon, Rainbow Gardens is full of novelties, oddities, and collectibles. Visit Planet Rainbow for gift selections of authentic Utah gifts and Olympic memorabilia.

Ume Design. 186 Historic 25th St.; (801) 393-7326; www.umedesigns.com. If you are looking for chic, don't look any further. This fashion store was named the Best Boutique in the Best of the Beehive Awards. Not only do they offer unique and stylish women's clothing, but also handbags and gifts. They even have a Happy Planet Place area dedicated to many organic, environmentally friendly products. Open Mon through Sat 11 a.m. to 6 p.m.

where to eat

El Matador Restaurante and Cantina. 2564 Ogden Ave.; (801) 393-3151; http://elmatador ogden.com. You might mistake this charming place for the Alamo as they have reconstructed a wall of the fortress, along with a little village that has the "south of the border" feel. If you're in love with chips and salsa, you could eat theirs by the bucketful. You will leave having had a truly wonderful experience and you might even pick up some of the language. Open 7 days a week starting at 11 a.m. $

Prairie Schooner Steakhouse. 445 Park Blvd.; (801) 621-5511 or (801) 392-2712; http://prairieschoonerrestaurant.com. Serving up some of the "meanest" steak, seafood, chicken, and prime rib this side of the Rockies, they will have you saying "Howdy, partner" before the evening is out. The Prairie Schooner makes you feel as though you are truly in the Wild West as you dine in a covered wagon next to an open prairie fire. $$–$$$

Roosters Brewing Company and Restaurant. 253 Historic 25th St.; (801) 627-6171; http://roostersbrewingco.com. You will find this to be one of the best gathering places for amazing cuisine, great conversation, and a relaxed atmosphere with an eclectic vibe. Enjoy the unique ambience and outdoor patio, for those beautiful summer evenings and fabulous fall days. You must try the blackened salmon sandwich—our mouths are still watering over that lunch. $

Rovali's Ristorante Italiano. 174 Historic 25th St.; (801) 394-1070; www.rovalis.com. You will soon be saying "grazie" after enjoying a delicious meal made from one of chef Ro's many homemade recipes. You will feel as though you have just landed in Italy, and it will leave you wanting more. Most nights they have live music to enjoy as you take in the tastes and smells of this appetizing journey. $

Sonora Grill. 2310 South Kiesel Ave.; (801) 393-1999; www.thesonoragrill.com. Here is a unique type of regional Mexican cuisine, including Utah's first ever ceviche bar. (Ceviche is seafood marinated and "cooked" in the juices of acidic fruit, and very popular in Latin America.) As you sit down with your appetizers, with chips and assorted salsas, you can really relax at and enjoy the ceviche bar, the full bar, lounge, or the main dining area. The food has an unparalleled freshness and does wonders to please your palate. We truly enjoyed the green salsa they serve before every meal. "Fabuloso!" Open Mon through Thurs 11 a.m. to 10 p.m., Fri and Sat 11 a.m. to 11 p.m., and Sun 11 a.m. to 9 p.m. $

Tona Sushi Bar and Grill. 210 Historic 25th St.; (801) 622-8662; www.tonarestaurant .com. You will definitely feel pampered as you experience the culinary delights that take place here. Sit at the sushi bar and watch the chef's creations unfold, or dine in the main area—the socks-only guest room. Open Tues through Sat. $

Union Grill. 2501 Wall Ave.; (801) 621-2830; www.uniongrillogden.com. After almost 20 years, family-friendly Union Grill in Historic Union Station has some of the most scrumptious cookery you will find. Assorted and healthy, but truly delightful, this is a place you won't want to miss. Open Mon through Thurs 11 a.m. to 10 p.m., Fri and Sat 11 a.m. to 10:30 p.m. $

where to stay

Alaskan Inn. 435 Ogden Canyon Rd.; (801) 621-8600; www.alaskaninn.com. You know you are in Utah, we know that you are in Utah, but at the Alaskan Inn bed-and-breakfast you will think you have just stepped into another place—namely, the arctic tundra. The inn reflects the crystal-crowned mountains, undisturbed wildlife, and miles of silent, extraordinary beauty of wide open Alaska. The 23 polar-inspired themed suites and cabins will give you the tranquility and relaxation you are looking for—and maybe a little romance, too! $$$

Ben Lomond Suites. 2510 Washington Blvd.; (877) 627-1900; www.benlomondsuites .com. At the heart of downtown Ogden you will find this jewel of a hotel. Ben Lomond was formerly known as the luxurious Bigelow Hotel. One of only three "grand hotels" in Utah, it is to this day the largest hotel in Ogden. The Italian Renaissance Revival style will draw you in and take you back to the glorious 1920s. All of the suites and condos have immense sitting rooms and bed chambers, which are perfect for business travelers or families. Come stay for while and step back in time. $$$

day trip 03

north

>>> **cute birds in hot water:**
willard, perry, brigham city,
honeyville

It has been said that there are adventures around every corner, but in this case they are just up the road. Well, about 52 miles up the road, that is. Just over an hour's drive north of Salt Lake City are the towns of Willard, Perry, Brigham City, and Honeyville. Slip off the freeway (I-15), and immerse yourself in miles of the most beautiful orchard country in the nation. Beneath the setting of the rugged peaks of the Wasatch Mountain Range, you will find myriad activities for your day trip. If you love fresh fruit, recreating at a nearly 10,000-acre freshwater lake sitting atop of the Great Salt Lake, or the discoveries of a 72,000-acre migratory bird refuge that is home to over 200 species of birds, this is a day trip you will want to visit over and over again. Of course, it just might be the year-round swimming in the soothing mineral bath of Crystal Hot Springs that keeps you coming back. Whether it is a single-day activity or a combination of many, the splendor and beauty of northern Utah is unmatched.

willard

Willard is really more of a starting place to begin your adventures as you enter Box Elder County. Beautiful scenery and the most incredible sunrises over mountains that look like towers of granite are only surpassed by the beautiful sunsets over the northern parts of the Great Salt Lake. Willard is mostly a small farming community but is also home to Willard Bay State Park and to the famous Smith & Edwards, which is a must see. (Where else can you possibly get a glimpse of, let alone purchase, a military tank for sale?)

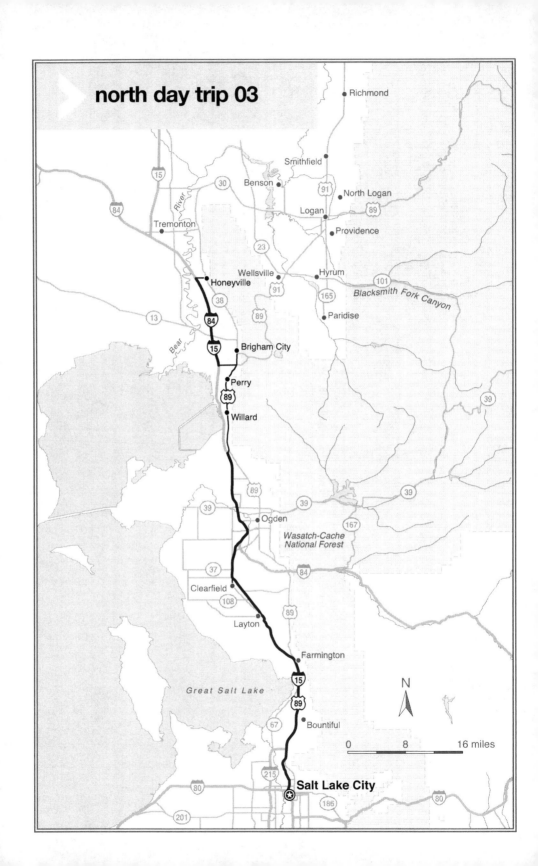

north day trip 03

Willard is a 1-mile strip of land that is trapped between the lake and Cache National Forest, which keeps the pace of life a bit slower. Here you will most likely share the road with local tractors, and the only traffic jams are when the local cows decide to wander.

getting there

Take I-15 north, 53 miles out of Salt Lake (about an hour). Take exit 351 for the South Bay and Smith & Edwards, or exit 357 for the North Bay and the main entrance to the state park.

where to go

Willard Bay State Park. Sitting atop of the Great Salt Lake, Willard Bay State Park is a boating and a fisherman's paradise. Nearly 10,000 acres of freshwater make it the perfect spot for waterskiing and boating enthusiasts. If you have a boat, bring it; if you don't, you can rent them through the park's concession service, Club Rec North at www.clubrec north.com.

Willard Bay is also one of the few lakes in Utah that doesn't freeze completely over in the harsh Utah winters. This provides year-round fishing for some of the state's best crappie, walleye, catfish, and wiper. It also creates the perfect environment in the winter for the nesting of American bald eagles, which take advantage of the open water to fish. Just to the south of Willard Bay are the Willard Bay Upland Game Management Area and the Harold S. Crane State Waterfowl Management Area.

Smith & Edwards. As you take exit 351 you will find a shopping experience that is a bit of a northern Utah novelty and an attraction itself. Smith & Edwards makes the claim that if they don't have it, you don't need it, and they have it all. The 171,000-square-foot store first started out as an assortment of military surplus and still has a 60-acre yard filled with everything from nuts and bolts to entire military vehicles. We offer a suggestion: Drop Dad and the boys off here and the rest of you take a drive through the orchards to pick up some fruit for the picnic on the shores of Willard Bay. Make sure you have a tracking device on the men you left behind, though—they will be tough to find.

where to eat

Note: For the most part this is a "bring your own" kind of location. There is 1 restaurant near the north park entrance, however, and others in Brigham City. (See Brigham City's "where to eat" section.)

Country Market. 600 W. 750 North; (435) 723-5022. Breakfast through dinner, you can choose from items such as their famous country-fried steak and eggs, flavorful taco salad, corned beef Reuben sandwich, or a USDA Choice rib eye steak. The atmosphere is family friendly and has that down-home feeling. For those looking for more variety in a meal, try the "bountiful buffet" with an ever-changing array of popular comfort foods and regional selections. A kids' menu is also available. $

where to stay

Willard Bay State Park. Overnight campgrounds in the park are **Cottonwood Camp-ground:** $25 (full hookups); **Willow Creek Campground:** $16; **South Marina Camp-ground:** $16.

perry

Check your brakes because you will be stopping a lot along this 10-mile stretch of US 89. This narrow strip of land produces some of the most delicious fruit ever grown. People travel from around the region every year to sample the "abundance of the best peaches in Utah." Spend the day at any of the pick-your-own stops; then slip beneath a willow tree on a hot, late summer day, close your eyes, and taste the sweetness of this lovely city.

After a day of savoring the "fruits" of your labors (or a day on the water), enjoy a night of entertainment in the historic Perry Heritage Community Theatre. Dedicated to quality family entertainment, you'll take pleasure in the charm and excitement of locally produced musicals, comedies, and dramas.

getting there

Go 52 miles north of Salt Lake City on I-15. Take exit 351. Stay to the right as you exit and merge with US 89 going north. Travel the 10-mile "fruit loop" (US 89) to Perry City.

where to go

The "Fruit Loop." Don't get too excited—you're not going to get your favorite breakfast cereal; rather, the best breakfast, lunch, or dinner Mother Nature can produce is found here by combining incredibly fertile soil with warm sunshine and a lot of hard work. Being uniquely protected by the mountains on the east and the more temperate atmosphere of a large body of water to the west make this the perfect place for growing the sweetest fruit in Utah.

Paul's Patch. 1894 S. US 89; (435) 723-7159. Opens in the spring and closes after Hal-loween. Enjoy your choice of shopping the roadside stand or picking your own produce. (Picking your own is so much fun and you get to be a bit more particular in your selection.) The workers are helpful, and of course everything is fresh! If you want a bit more variety than what is grown locally, they also bring in other fruits like oranges and bananas, along with other "out of season" produce.

Tagge's Famous Fruit. 3431 S US 89; (801) 755-8031. Maintaining more than 2,500 fruit trees and over 12,000 tomato plants on 30 acres, this an ideal place to stop for the fresh-est fruit around. Pick your own or buy from the local family growers in their fruit stand, the choice is yours. Picking your own will help you appreciate the long hours put in to putting food on the table. Don't forget the jams, jellies, preserves, variety of vegetables, or tomatoes from 1 of those 12,000 plants.

Heritage Community Theatre, Inc. 2505 S. US 89; www.heritagetheatreutah.com. Local community theater is one of the most enjoyable experiences, especially when it is of the caliber produced by Heritage Community Theatre. The setting seems more personal and less pompous. Set in a historic church built in 1890, the Heritage Community Theatre is a large 220-seat venue. One of the longest lasting theater groups, the Heritage Community Theatre produces plays throughout the year. There is something magical for a child or even an adult when the lights go down and the curtain goes up. Check their schedule and shows each season. This will surely be a return trip or maybe holiday tradition.

where to eat

Maddox Ranch House. 1900 S US 89, Brigham City; (435) 723-8545; www.maddox finefood.com. Located on the border of Perry and Brigham City, this is "one of the most popular eating places in Utah." Maddox Ranch House has a style and taste that is uniquely Utah. From upscale dining, to takeout, to an old-fashioned drive-in, Maddox has it all. Very generous portions and a reputation for the best beef make Maddox a local favorite. Specialties such as turkey steak, shrimp steak, and natural bison will keep you coming back every time you make this day trip. Open Tues through Sat 11 a.m. to 9 p.m. $–$$

brigham city

Peaceful is the word that best describes Brigham City. It is one of those towns that still have that "Mayberry" feel. Historic downtown and the newly refurbished Brigham City Depot create the illusion that you're stepping off the train 100 years ago. Whether you spend the day visiting the city's museums, art galleries, festivals, or historical places such as the Box Elder Tabernacle, or you take a scenic drive up the canyon to nearby Mantua Reservoir for a late afternoon swim, Brigham City has a little something for everyone.

getting there

Take I-15 north from Salt Lake City 55 miles to the 1100 South Brigham City exit. Keep right and follow it to the mouth of the canyon, where you will turn left on US 89, also known as SR 69, and by local street signs as Main Street.

where to go

Brigham City Museum-Gallery. 24 N. 300 West; (435) 723-6769. Open Mon through Fri 11 a.m. to 6 p.m. and Sat 1 to 5 p.m. Admission is free. This is a small-town museum and gallery that is unmatched in providing quality programming depicting the life and times of the region. Besides the rotating gallery and historic selection, it features 1 or 2 national traveling shows a year and exhibits by local Utah artists. It is rich in heritage, allowing both young and old to truly get a sense of how it was when Brigham City was first settled.

Box Elder Tabernacle. 251 S. Main St. This building is a perfect example of 19th-century Latter-day Saint architecture. Taking 32 years to complete due to hardship and a subsequent fire that burned everything but the stone walls in 1 hour, this structure is proof of the perseverance of the people who sacrificed to rebuild and dedicate it the following year (1897). It is one of the most beautiful tabernacles in the region, if not the state. Still in use as a meeting house for the Church of Jesus Christ of Latter-day Saints, the building is also available for tours daily.

Idle Isle Candy. 41 S. Main St.; (435) 723-8003; www.idleisle.com. Indulge yourself in history and delight in this small-town candy store. Find yourself returning to the 1920s when it was first opened and taste the results of time-tested, old-fashioned candy-making techniques still in use there today. Open Mon through Sat 10 a.m. to 7 p.m.

Bear River Migratory Bird Refuge. 2155 W. Forest St.; (435) 723-5887 (office), (435) 734-6425 (visitor information); www.fws.gov/bearriver. Located where the Bear River enters the Great Salt Lake, this tranquil oasis has the most unique waterfowl watching in the western United States. Start your journey at the Wildlife Education Center, which is west of the junction of Forest Street and I-15 (exit 363). Interact, become part of your surroundings, and then begin the 12-mile auto tour loop. You are sure to see plenty of wildlife, including the 55,000 American White Pelicans that make their home on the Great Salt Lake's Gunnison Island. This is one of America's largest pelican colonies. Wrap yourself in the sights and sounds of over 200 species of birds that make their way to the refuge. Any time of year is a great time to visit, including the winter, when you will see at least 1 of the 40,000 Tundra Swans often reported here. A refuge birding report, which is updated monthly, can be heard by calling (435) 734-6426.

where to eat

Idle Isle Cafe. 24 S. Main St.; (435) 734-2468. A local landmark, the Idle Isle Cafe will cap off your day in a very cool way. This dining experience in Brigham City is as unique as its building. After you dine, walk across the street and pick up some of their incredible candies to go. Open Mon through Sat 10 a.m. to 7 p.m. $

Maddox Ranch House. 1900 S. US 89; (435) 723-8545; www.maddoxfinefood.com. Located on the border of Perry and Brigham City, this place is repeated from a previous day trip because it is so good. It is also "one of the most popular eating places in Utah." Maddox Ranch House has a style and taste that is uniquely Utah. From upscale dining, to takeout, to an old-fashioned drive-in, Maddox has it all. Very generous portions and a reputation for the best beef make Maddox a local favorite. Specialties such as turkey steak, shrimp steak, and natural bison will keep you coming back on each day trip. Open Tues through Sat 11 a.m. to 9 p.m. $–$$

Wingers. 855 W. 1100 South (US 91); (435) 723-3910. This is a great place to eat and enjoy the company of family or friends after a day trip north. Wings are of course their specialty and are "amazing" with their Original Amazing Sauce. From the burgers to the salads, you can't go wrong here. The atmosphere is relaxed and popcorn is your appetizer—need we say more? Open Sun noon to 9 p.m., Mon through Thurs 11 a.m. to 10 p.m., and Sat and Sun 11 a.m. to 11 p.m. $

where to stay

Crystal Inn Hotel. 480 Westland Dr., Brigham City; (800) 408-0440. A great place at a great price, Crystal Inn provides that home-away-from-home feeling needed after a day in "Mayberry." Nice oversized rooms and suites provide space for everyone in your party. It is a good place to stay if you are planning on venturing further north the next day. $

Days Inn. 1033 S. 1600 West, Perry; (435) 723-3500. Located right off I-15 and exit 362, it is one of the area's newest hotels. Enjoy the complimentary Daybreak Breakfast and warm, friendly atmosphere before a restful night's sleep to ready for tomorrow's adventures. $

honeyville

With a population still less than 2,000, Honeyville remains a picturesque farming community sandwiched between the striking Wellsville Mountains to the east and the Bear River to the west. This scenic, sleepy town has some unique geological traits that provide both hot and cold mineral springs. Relax and enjoy the healing powers of both beauty and the elements of Crystal Hot Springs.

getting there

Take I-15 65 miles north to exit 372. Stay right then turn right on 6900 North (SR 240). At SR 38 (2800 West) turn left and travel north 1.7 miles to Crystal Hot Springs.

where to go

Crystal Hot Springs. 825 N. SR-38; (435) 279-8104; www.crystalhotsprings.net. Open year-round (10 a.m. to 10 p.m. in the summer and noon to 10 p.m. in the winter). Also note the waterslide is closed in the winter Mon through Fri. Play, and sit back and unwind in this natural wonder. Crystal Hot Springs is one of only two locations in the world where both natural hot and cold springs are found less than 50 feet apart. Emerging spontaneously from the core of the earth, these waters rejuvenate both body and soul. Originally used by Native Americans as a camp in the winter, it was rediscovered by the Chinese railroad workers building the transcontinental railroad. Just as in days of old, these waters provide a relaxing, muscle-soothing mineral bath; but unlike then, when the only "tubs" were handmade from cedarwood, today you can soak with modern conveniences and the fun of waterslides and an Olympic pool.

where to stay

Crystal Hot Springs Campground. 825 N. SR 38; (435) 279-8104; www.crystalhot springs.net. With over 100 campsites, some with full hookups ($25) and some with no hookups ($15), you are sure to find something that fits your needs. Conveniently located at the Hot Springs, this makes it easy to stay as long as you wish. $

day trip 04

north

wild, wild west of the north:
south cache valley, wellsville,
paradise, providence

south cache valley

Whether you are in for a downright ugly shoot 'em up shoot-out or some relaxation and peace, you will find both extremes within the beautiful Cache Valley. Originally named Willow Valley because of the huge number of willows growing along its myriad rivers and streams, the name ended up being changed to Cache Valley for the fact that the early fur trappers would cache (or hide) their furs in the surrounding area. In French the word *cache* (pronounced *cash*) means "to hide or store one's treasure." Cache Valley definitely has "hidden treasures" for those looking for outdoor adventures, hands-on Wild West experiences, and fine and performing arts. Within the ageless beauty and seasons of Cache Valley, you will find that you can go snowmobiling in the morning and ride a Jet Ski in the afternoon, if you pick the right day.

Cache Valley is surrounded by impressively beautiful yet rugged mountains. Hiking, bird watching, rock climbing, canoeing, mountain biking, water sporting, snowmobiling, skiing, and snowshoeing are just a few of the outdoor attractions.

getting there

Drive north on I-15 about 55 miles to exit 362, Brigham City 1100 South. Continue on US 91/US 89 26 miles. US 91 will take you to the heart of Cache Valley. Keep a lookout as you will pass by Sherwood Hills Resort before you exit the canyon.

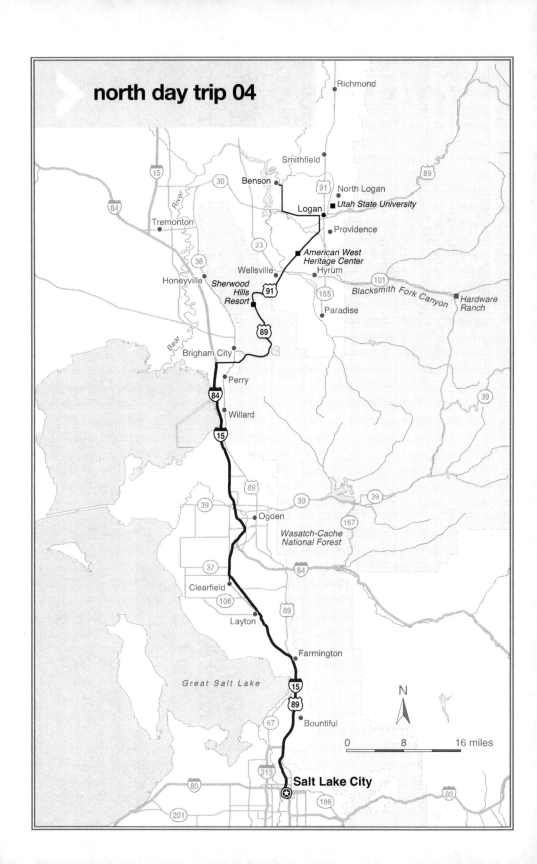

north day trip 04

where to go

Sherwood Hills Resort and Spa. Sherwood Hills Resort is located on US 89/91 in Sardine Canyon between Logan (10½ miles) and Brigham City (11 miles) at 7877 So. US 89/91, Wellsville; (435) 245-5054; www.sherwoodhills.com. This year-round resort and spa can be found nestled up against the distinguished Wellsville Mountains intertwined within Sardine Canyon. Enjoy a 9-hole round of golf with the backdrop of the steepest mountains watching over you. Everything from hiking, mountain biking, swimming, bird watching, tennis, and volleyball is available. The annual Wimmer's XC Mountain Bike Race takes place at Sherwood Hills Resort. Try the trails that would challenge some of the most experienced bikers, or just enjoy the paved paths that will allow you to take in the amazing and pristine atmosphere. When you are done, finish your day in their new European-Style Spa, where they offer a variety of refreshing and rejuvenating services to relax.

For winter enthusiasts, there are many day activities, including cross-country skiing and snowshoeing through some of the most stunning terrain in Northern Utah. There are at least 2 miles of trails that you can enjoy no matter how experienced a skier you are. They also have a wonderfully inviting restaurant that will thrill your taste buds with Old World charm. You will feel as though you just landed in an Italian villa where you will come away with *amore di cibo*—a love for food. Among the many things baked fresh daily are their breads, pastries, and desserts. This is not only a recreation destination but a wonderful place to plan an extended stay for any special occasion or to unwind. They have many rooms to choose from and several are newly remodeled.

American West Heritage Center. Just as you descend out of Sardine Canyon at the base of the beautiful Wellsville Mountains, you will find one of Utah's favorite living history farms on 160 acres at 4025 S. US 89/91 in Wellsville; (435) 245-6050; www.awhc.org. Discover what life must have been like on the western frontier from 1820 to1920. If you are in the mood for some old-fashioned fun, they fill the year with a fantastic array of family activities such as: The Haunted Hollow, handcart treks (our family really enjoyed the adventurous feeling of pulling our own cart and having to eat a true cowpoke dinner), summer camps, Daily Summer Adventures, festivals, scout and youth days, Baby Animal Days, and Fall Harvest Days. The center touts turn-of-the-century farming and farm life with mountain men, Native Americans, and pioneers. Take a wagon ride around the farm, pet the animals, ride a train, try your hand at washing dishes, tour the old farmhouse, taste a Dutch oven dinner, throw a hatchet, mine for gold, listen to old time stories, make arts and crafts, visit a Native American village or Old West town, see a mountain man rendezvous site, or tap your toes to the western entertainment. Hours of operation vary depending on the season and special events, so call for more details.

Hardware Ranch. Hardware Ranch is located about 15 miles east of Hyrum on SR 101, in Blacksmith Fork Canyon; (435) 753-6206 or 753-6168; www.http://wildlife.utah.gov/ hardwareranch. The State of Utah purchased this land to operate a winter feeding program for Rocky Mountain elk. Hardware Ranch Wildlife Management Area (WMA) also provides habitat for many other species of wildlife and promotes wildlife research and management, plus a host of other outdoor activities for the outdoor enthusiast. Hardware Ranch offers pleasurable opportunities during the winter months, including horse-drawn sleigh rides to view the winter elk, snowmobiling, sledding, a winter holiday celebration during Dec, and the autumn Elk Festival (which includes free wagon rides, pumpkin painting, shooting games, antler balloons, and more). During other times of the year, there are prospects for fishing, camping, and recreational hunting during the appropriate hunting seasons. There are elk, moose, ruffed grouse, chukar, and cottontail rabbits that can all be hunted on the 14,000-acre management area. Hardware Ranch has a restaurant offering a large selection of meals, a coffee shop, and a gift shop, but call first as they are only open certain times of the year.

Canoeing the Bear River. There are 2 main boat launches that are available: **Benson Marina,** located on 3000 North and approximately 4800 West, near Benson and **Cutler Marsh Marina,** located on 200 North and approximately 4800 West, a few miles west of downtown Logan. **The best places to rent canoes for your outdoor adventure:**

- **Muddy Road Outfitters Canoe Rentals.** 4705 W. 3800 North, Benson; (435) 753-3693. Muddy Road Outfitters will let you "play in their backyard" (the Cutler Reservoir is right behind their farm) for only $15 a day per each canoe, or they will meet you at the Ballard Bridge with the canoes and drive your vehicle back to their house, where you will end your 2½-hour float trip. Canoes are $25 a day or $20 a day if you rent 3 or more. They can fit 2 adults (and 1 to 2 small kids) and come with life jackets and other items for your outdoor sightseeing adventure. Come prepared to take lots of pictures as you never know what you may encounter. Sandhill cranes, great blue herons, snowy egrets, Canada geese, white pelicans, common egrets, western grebes, and many more species of birds are all possibilities.

- **Utah State University Outdoor Recreation.** 1050 N. 950 East., Utah State University Campus, Logan; (435) 797-3264; www.usu.edu/orc. They offer much more than just canoes for rental so give them a call or check out their website to see the plethora of items they have available for your outdoor adventure. One popular canoeing area is called the Cutler Wetlands Maze, where you can get lost amongst the cattails. Information and maps are available at the website www.bridgerlandaudobon.org/wetlands maze. Call for hours of operation and seasonal adventures.

Cache Valley Hunter Education Center. 2851 W. 200 North (3 miles west of Logan on Garland Highway), Logan; (435) 753-4600. If you are in the mood for an organized and safe shooting experience, give this a try. Their classes and facilities include: indoor pistol; outdoor pistol to 50 yards; practical pistol; indoor rifle, outdoor rifle to 100 yards; black powder; trap; skeet; sporting clay, archery, and air guns. Open Wed, Thurs, and Fri 9 a.m. to 5 p.m. and Sat 3 to 8 p.m.

where to shop

American West Heritage Center. 4025 South US 89/91, Wellsville; (435) 245-6050; www.awhc.org. This authentic Old Western town touts a country store that holds many fun treasures including handmade quilts, old candies, toys, etc. Yee-haw! You will feel like you have gone back in time at least 100 years. Inside their main building is the gift shop that features Utah-made, Native American, and western items for sale.

Cox Honeyland Gift Shop. 1780 S. US 89/91, Logan; (435) 752-3234; www.coxhoney .com. This flavorful and mouthwatering store can be found just a few minutes south of Logan. If you thought that honey was just for eating, let Cox Honeyland show you many other honey-based gifts including lotions, candles, massage bars, and various other items. You'll want to wander in this store a while as you browse the amazing wares, and even observe a live, glass-enclosed beehive.

Weeks Berries of Paradise. 8650 S. 800 East, Paradise; (435) 245-3377. Stop by to purchase their amazing products, but call first to make sure they are in from the fields. This family business is owned and operated by Mervin Weeks, who bought 2 acres of land after graduating from horticulture school in 1978. Because of the perfect growing conditions for their berries, they produce raspberries, blueberries, currants, blackberries, strawberries, and gooseberries. After 27 years in operation, they have shared many healthy and incredible gourmet items with their neighbors as well as the general public. These are just few of their delicious products: freezer jam, gourmet jams and syrups, and healthy, bold and unique tasting juices from their currants and raspberries.

where to eat

Casper's Malt Shoppe. 585 W. 100 North, Suite 1, Providence; (435) 713-0056. Open daily except Sun. This has the feel of a small-town malt shop. Whether you want a shake, ice-cream cone, banana split, malt, or one of their famous "Fat Boys," you will truly enjoy every minute of your ice-cream adventure. They also have a 10-minute video presentation that shares their history and the secret process behind their famously wonderful frozen perfections. $

Cracker Barrel Cafe & Catering. 8990 S. SR 65, Paradise; (435) 245-4258. Don't get this restaurant confused with the national chain. This local Cracker Barrel has been around here for many years, first as a ZCMI store, and has recently been remodeled. The country atmosphere will surely take you back a few years to "Mayberry," and the food will fill any country dish wish you might have. They are known throughout Utah for their indescribably delectable prime rib, which they cook in a special oven overnight. (No, they are not giving out their secret recipe—we asked!) They have a "fish bowl" kitchen, which means it's an open kitchen where you can watch the chef preparing your food while you talk with him about his "secret recipe." They also have fresh homemade baked goods. Open Mon to Sat from 6 a.m. to 9 p.m. $

Firehouse Pizzeria. 880 S. Main St., Logan; (435) 787-4222; firehousepizzeria.com. If you want an eclectic atmosphere with enticing smells coming from the pizza oven, this is the place for you. They have a wide selection of original and outlandish pizza combinations, pastas (veggie lovers and gluten free), calzones, salads, etc. Need a good laugh? They have a Comedy Club on Fri evenings with an all-you-can-eat dinner starting at 9:30 p.m. Open Mon to Thurs from 11 a.m. to 10 p.m. and Fri and Sat from 11 a.m. to 11 p.m. $

Old Grist Mill Bread Co. 981 S. Main St., Logan; (435) 755-0262. Their main store is located at 78 E. 400 North, Logan; (435) 753-6463. If you want a hearty and healthy sit-down meal, you can visit the south store and choose to dine in or take out. They have a large selection of fresh bread (their specialty), and sandwiches, soups, bagels, pastries, etc. They use only the best and freshest ingredients so you might feel as though you are back at Grandma's house enjoying her home cooking. The raspberry and cinnamon rolls melt in your mouth. The south store is open Mon through Thurs from 8:30 a.m. to 8 p.m. and Fri and Sat from 8:30 a.m. to 8:30 p.m. $

South Cache Valley is limited in the area of places to shop, eat, and sleep. Please check out the Logan section for greater selections of all of the above.

where to stay

Providence Inn Bed and Breakfast. 10 South Main, Providence; (435) 752-3432 or (800) 480-4943; www.providenceinn.com. The Old Rock Church has a certain ambience, as it was once an old meetinghouse that is nestled in the serene community of Providence, only minutes from downtown Logan. The church was built by the Mormon pioneers in 1871. Attached to the church is the Providence Inn, which provides a romantic getaway or business retreat for small conferences. They have an array of interesting and adventuresome rooms, such as the Cape Cod Cottage, the Mountain Stream Room, the New Orleans Room, and Monet's Garden, to name a few. A made-to-order hot breakfast is included. $

day trip 05

north

>>> **say "cheese" at the opera**
logan, cache valley

Breathtakingly beautiful and with a rich tradition for various arts, entertainment, and festivals, Logan is home to the Utah Festival Opera and is a showcase for theater, ballet, and opera throughout the year. Drive up early and stroll among the unique shops along Main Street. Step back in time as you enter the landmark Bluebird Restaurant to one of the few remaining authentic soda fountains, dine on the popular Bluebird Chicken, and check out the handmade chocolates.

Originally founded in 1859, Cache Valley was an early outpost for the fur trappers. It quickly grew into a region rich in agriculture as the pioneers came in search of fertile ground. Today Logan is home to Utah State University. Originally the state agricultural college, it has since grown into a major research and learning center. USU is one of the most beautiful campuses and should be a part of any visit to Logan.

Set on the hill overlooking the city is the historic Logan LDS Temple, which was finished in 1884. It stands as a monument to Logan's pioneer heritage and the continuing dedication of faithful Latter-day Saints to this city.

When you look beyond Main Street, you will find rare treasures hidden in many of the small towns of Cache Valley. Restaurants, shops, and cafes are among the few tucked away in Logan's backstreets and alleyways.

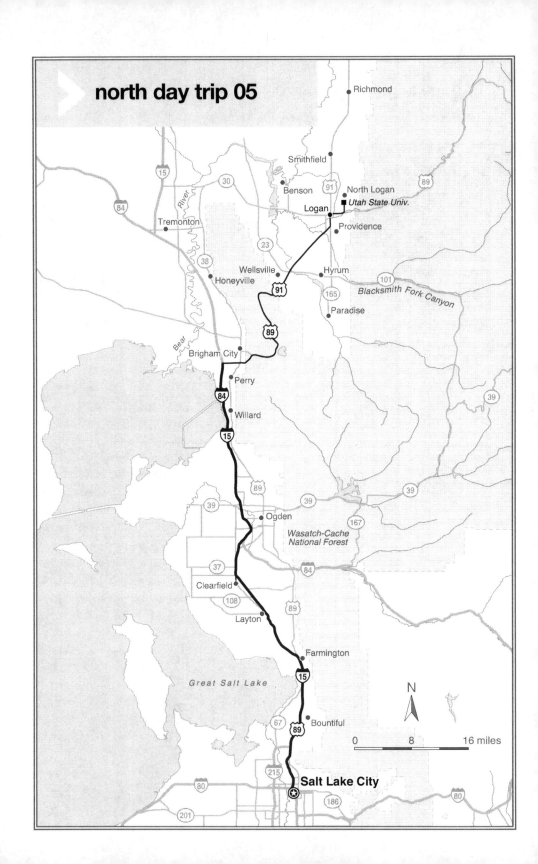

north day trip 05

Richmond

Smithfield

Benson

North Logan

Logan

Utah State Univ.

Providence

Tremonton

Wellsville

Hyrum

Honeyville

Paradise

Blacksmith Fork Canyon

Brigham City

Perry

Willard

Ogden

Wasatch-Cache
National Forest

Clearfield

Layton

Farmington

Great Salt Lake

Bountiful

N

0   8   16 miles

Salt Lake City

getting there

Drive north about 55 miles to exit 362, Brigham City 1100 South. Continue on US 91/US 89 26 miles, following the signs to Logan. US 91 will take you to Main Street and Logan's downtown. The canyon (Sardine) is breathtaking in autumn, the end of Sept through the middle of Oct being the best time for fall foliage.

where to go

Cache Valley Visitors Bureau. 199 N. Main St.; (435) 755-1890 or (800) 882-4433; www .tourcachevalley.com. If you want extended information on Logan and the Cache Valley area, the staff at the Cache Valley Visitors Bureau will be more than happy to answer any questions by phone or in person. Their website has a plethora of information for accommodations, shopping, dining, outdoor recreation, transportation, hot getaway deals, arts, entertainment, and a calendar of events.

Ellen Eccles Theatre. Cache Valley Center for the Arts, 43 S. Main St.; (435) 752-0026; www.centerforthearts.us. The prestigious Ellen Eccles Theatre was built by the Thatcher family and opened in 1923 as the Capitol Theatre. After falling into disrepair, it was eventually restored by the community and reopened as the breathtaking and majestic theater you see today. As you enter this elegant and plush edifice, it will seem as though you have just stepped back in time. Take notice of the detailed woodwork and gold trim.

Since its renovation the Ellen Eccles Theatre has been the center of artistic activity in Cache Valley. Throughout the summer, Utah Festival Opera offers world-renowned operas and other musical masterpieces. The performances you will encounter at Ellen Eccles will rival anything that you would see on Broadway in New York City. From Sept to May the Cache Valley Center for the Arts presents a variety of touring Broadway productions and premier artists that bring cultural enlightenment, enrichment, and an amazingly diverse assortment of performances to the community. Throughout the year you can catch performances from many other local arts organizations, including Cache Regional Theatre Company, Valley Dance Ensemble, and Cache Valley Civic Ballet, among others.

The Dansante. 59 S. 100 West; (435) 750-0300; www.ufoc.org. The Dansante Building has played an important role in the social life of the Cache Valley community since 1900. For many years it served as the valley's premier dance hall, and during significant holidays it has been known to host up to 3,000 people. This beautiful building was renovated when purchased by the Utah Festival Opera Company. Now it speaks volumes about those who have worked or do work within these walls and their upmost respect and love for the arts. It hosts a 124-seat recital hall, rehearsal halls, practice rooms, plus a plethora of props, makeup, costumes, and a scene shop.

Old Lyric Repertory Company. 28 W. Center St.; (435) 797-8022. This historic 1913 Caine Lyric Theatre is one of the few remaining true repertory companies in the US. You will

cache valley food tour

Did someone say "Cheese, please!"? Cache Valley is known for many things, among them the big variety of cheeses—and who doesn't love cheese? Known as the "land of milk and honey," Cache Valley truly knows how to show off its wares. While visiting the food factories, you will be able to sample some of the incredible cheeses, milk products, coffee, honey, cookies, and chocolates. For more information call (435) 755-1890 or visit www.tourcachevalley.com.

Here is a list of the companies excited to have you visit:

Aggie Ice Cream & True Blue Cheese. *Utah State University; Nutrition & Food Science Building; 750 N. 1200 East, Logan; (435) 797-2109; Mon to Fri 9 a.m. to 10 p.m., Sat 10 a.m. to 10 p.m. Tour: 1:30 p.m. Mon through Fri.*

Bluebird Candy Factory. *75 W. Center St., Logan; (435) 753-3670; Mon through Sat 10 a.m. to 5 p.m. Tour: 11 a.m. Mon, Tues, and Wed (Memorial Day to Labor Day).*

Cafe Ibis. *52 Federal Ave., Logan; (435) 753-4777; open daily, hours vary; gourmet coffees. Tour: 3 p.m., Mon through Sat.*

Crumb Brothers Artisan Bread. *"Best Bakery in Utah," Salt Lake Magazine, 2008; 291 S. 300 West, Logan; (435) 792-6063. Tour: 9:30 a.m. Mon through Thurs.*

Gardeners Markets. *Pioneer Park, 200 E. 100 South; (435) 755-3950; art, music, and fresh homegrown produce; Sat 9 a.m. to 1 p.m., mid-May to mid-Oct.*

Harvest Market at Rockhill Creamery. *200 E. 100 South, Richmond; fresh homegrown produce; Sat 10 a.m. to 2 p.m., mid-May to mid-Oct.*

Rockhill Creamery. *563 S. State St., Richmond; (435) 258-1278; Sat 10 a.m. to 2 p.m. Cache Valley's Micro Dairy Tour: Sat 10 a.m. to 2 p.m., mid-Apr to mid-Oct.*

Here are few other places you may enjoy:

Alvey's Candies. *Cache Valley Mall, 1300 N. Main St., Logan; (435) 753-8888.*

Gossner Foods. *1000 W. 1000 North, Logan; (435) 752-9365.*

Heart to Heart Foods, Inc. *142 W. 3200 North, Hyde Park; (435) 753-9602.*

Lower Foods. *700 S. US 91, Richmond; (435) 258-2449.*

Pepperidge Farm Outlet Store. *901 N. 200 West, Richmond; (435) 258-2491.*

find the same cast whether they present a mystery, comedy, musical, or drama. Open the end of June through the first week in Aug.

Logan River Golf Course. 550 W. 1000 South; (435) 750-0123, (888) 750-0123; www .loganutah.org/parks_and_rec. Logan River is an 18-hole, par 71 golf course, and it is a favorite for not only locals but visitors, too. There are various annual tournaments that the Golf Division hosts, while sustaining men's and women's leagues as well as junior camp programs.

Logan Aquatic Center. 451 S. 500 West; (435) 716-9266 or (435) 716-9280. www.logan utah.org/parks_and_rec. If the weather is warm and inviting, what could be better than a splash in a pool and boomeranging down a slide with your kids? (It may even make you feel young again.) The Logan Aquatic Center can be a full day of fun with a 50-meter lap pool, diving pool with a low and high dive, 2 waterslides, and a leisure/kiddy pool for the children with water depth ranging from 6 inches to 3 feet and water "mushrooms" to swim under to your kids' absolute delight. They offer an extensive list of classes: swimming lessons, water aerobics, a hydrofit class, lap swimming, fit for life seniors, and Boy Scouts of America merit badge classes. There are plenty of lounge chairs and picnic tables with umbrellas. If you want to come and just enjoy the sun while the kids swim, there is a grassy area that's great for sunbathing or having a picnic. *Note:* The Logan Aquatic Center will not open if the outside temperature is below 65 degrees.

Utah State University. 4300 Old Main Hill; (435) 797-0017 or (800) 231-5634. Utah State has a historic campus that touts an academic ambience of well-rounded students. With exceptional student involvement, museums, activities, athletics, performances, etc., the opportunities are endless. Here are a few of the possibilities:

The Utah State University Ropes Course. Utah State University, 5005 Old Main Hill; (435) 797-0089 or (800) 538-2663; www.ropes.usu.edu. There's no better way to have a fun, educational approach to learning and applying real life principles than at the Utah State University Ropes Course. The USU Ropes Course is better known as the Challenge Course, Confidence Course, or COPE Course. It can be used for businesses, families, church groups, and more. There are 3 sections: initiative games, low elements, and high course elements. Initiative games are problem-solving activities on the ground that require brainstorming and teamwork. Low course elements are from the ground level up to 4 feet off the ground and are definitely more challenging physically. The low elements require communication, group effort, trust, and, of course, cooperation. High course elements range from 12 to 50 feet up in the air and are considered high adventure activities. The high elements focus mainly on individual accomplishments that require team camaraderie. Everyone who participates is required to wear a harness and helmet. Open 9 a.m. to 6 p.m. or dusk, Mon to Sat.

Nora Eccles Harrison Museum of Art. 650 N. 1100 East; (435) 797-0163; http://art
museum.usu.edu. The Nora Eccles Harrison Museum of Art encompasses one of the
largest art collections in the Intermountain West, including a great assortment of Native
American artwork.

USU Chase Fine Arts Center. 4030 Old Main Hill; (435) 797-3040; www.usu.edu/finearts.
The Chase Fine Arts Center is located on the southeast corner of the Utah State University
campus. When coming into Cache Valley from the north or south, turn east from Main Street
onto 400 North and continue up the hill until you reach 1200 East. The Chase Fine Arts
Center is located on the corner of 400 North and 1200 East, The Chase Fine Arts Center
includes the Kent Concert Hall, Morgan Theatre, Caine Lyric Theatre, Performance Hall,
Tippetts Exhibit Hall, and Black Box Studio Theatre. There is always some sort of magic
going on at one of these venues.

Aggie Ice Cream. On the corner of 700 North 1200 East (on the campus at USU); (435)
797-1000; www.aggieicecream.usu.edu. Come try some of the famous Aggie Ice Cream,
known worldwide for its amazing taste. After a trip to enjoy an activity or performance at
Utah State University, you can check out the variety of flavors and specialties that will tickle
your taste buds. You may never want to leave!

Logan Canyon National Scenic Byway. (435) 755-1890; www.logancanyon.com. The
Logan Canyon National Scenic Byway offers plenty of extreme natural beauty, varying
recreational opportunities, and amazing tales to satisfy even the most demanding adventurer. This route can be traveled by bicycle, foot, or car. Whichever you choose, you'll have
a truly wonderful story to share. The road will take you through colorful and enchanting
patches of wildflowers, bushes, and trees, as you wind around steep cliffs of limestone
and along picturesque streams bursting with trout. Located approximately 90 miles north
of Salt Lake City, this stretch of US 89 runs from the city of Logan to the clear blue waters
of Bear Lake. Just before entering Logan Canyon, you will find the grassy park that marks
the first of three dams, First Dam. On a beautiful, sunny day you will find the banks alive
with activity: sunbathers, volleyball, picnickers, and, of course, college students. If you are
willing to share your food, you will make many friends with the local geese and ducks.
There are plenty of places to plant your fishing poles in hopes of catching one of the fish
that are stocked here.

where to shop

DownEast Outfitters Home and Clothing. 1050 N. Main St.; (435) 787-4109; DownEast
Basics: www.downeastbasics.com. Here is a shopping experience that can give you
name-brand clothing and furniture without the name-brand prices, including their popular
DownEast Basics clothing line. They have clothing for women, children, and men.

Magical Moon Toys. 1451 N. 200 East, Suite 190; (435) 752-8697; www.magicalmoon toys.com. This store will make you want to be a kid again! At this destination in itself, you could spend the better part of the afternoon just browsing the copious treasures on hand. It has the largest selection of toys in northern Utah and sells a host of great treats: fresh fudge, caramel corn, taffy, and other delights. Good luck getting the kids to leave.

On the Avenue. Historic downtown Logan; 34 Federal Ave.; (435) 753-1150. As you walk in, you will smell the candles that bring up thoughts of seasons past. With an eclectic array of merchandise including everything from soaps and lotions to crafts, home decor, and treats, On the Avenue will give you diverse options for gift giving or something special just for you.

Sugar 'n Spice Home Decor. 909 S. Main St., Suite D; (435) 753-6446 and 3655 N. US 91, Hyde Park; (435) 563-3206; www.sugarnspiceyourhome.com. If you are looking for a craft boutique that has the trendy feel, you have found your place. They sell wreaths, gar- lands, containers, baskets, seasonal decor, and much, much more!

where to eat

Angie's Restaurant. 690 N. Main St.; (435) 752-9252. This place has been around for many years, and some of the customers come in every day just for "the usual." Angie's is known as the place "Where the Locals Eat." This has a real down-home, country feel, where the smells of homemade pies and pastries make you want to linger until you are famished enough to try it all. If you are in the mood to challenge your vacationing buddies, you can dig into the big ice-cream bowl that looks like a sink filled to the brim with 3 different kinds of ice cream, various topping, bananas, and whipping cream. If you can finish it off, they will give you a car sticker that reads "I cleaned the sink at Angie's." $

The Beehive Grill. 255 S. Main St.; (435) 753-2600; www.thebeehivegrill.com. If you want some of the best root beer around, you have to try The Beehive Grill, Logan's first root beer brew pub. As you walk in, you must pass the freshly made gelato, and it will be truly hard to think about lunch or dinner at that point, but you cannot pass up the astounding quality and diverse choices inside the restaurant. The Beehive Grill offers a variety of mainly upscale recipes, mixed with some old favorites. You will not be disappointed as you enjoy the ambi- ence of a new-style brewery. Open daily at 11:30 a.m. for lunch and dinner. $

Cafe Sabor. 600 W. Center St.; (435) 752-8088; www.cafesabor.com. *"Olé!"* (which means "Bravo!") is the first reaction you will have after tempting your taste buds with all the amazing things to eat at this restaurant that touts food from "south of the border." As you start with their well-known salsa, make sure that you save room for the food, as it does not come in small portions. If you are in the mood to sit on their outdoor but covered patio, just put in your request. Cafe Sabor is the perfect recipe for your cravings—it has the ideal mix of flavors that complement one another. Check their website for dates of live entertainment. Open Mon through Thurs 11 a.m. to 10 p.m. and Fri and Sat 11 a.m. to 11 p.m. $

Caffe Ibis. Historic Downtown Logan, 52 Federal Ave.; (435) 753-4777; www.caffeibis .com. Caffe Ibis is not only owned and operated by family, but it is an award-winning "Green Business" and artisan custom coffee roasting house. Founded in 1976, their focus is on triple certified, organic, fair trade, and Smithsonian shade-grown, "bird-friendly" coffee from around the world. Along with the award-winning custom coffee company, they also operate an award-winning Gallery Deli with a full-service espresso bar. You'll also find weekly live music shows here to accompany your mode of relaxation. $

Elements. 640 S. 35 East; (435) 750-5170; http://theelementsrestaurant.com. Elements serves contemporary American cuisine with a taste and presentation that could rival any peak-performing metropolitan restaurant. It has a relaxing and warm atmosphere that is also elegant. As you sit by the little brook outside on the veranda behind the restaurant, you'll feel as though you are far from the city. The food presentation not only looks like an art masterpiece but is like heaven to the palate. Open Mon though Thurs 11 a.m. to 9 p.m. and Fri through Sat from 11 a.m. to 10 p.m. $$

Great Harvest Bread Co. 55 W. Center St.; (435) 787-4442. Plain and simple, this place is known for its down-to-earth baking philosophy with fresh ingredients and whole grains. If you want some warm soup and hot bread to take the edge off a winter day, this is a great place. You have the option to dine in or take out, but whatever you choose, you will be satisfied. They also offer a wide array of baked goods. Walk in and see if you can resist! $

Hamiltons Steak and Seafood. 2427 N. Main St.; (435) 787-8450; www.hamiltons steakhouse.com. If you are looking for a delicious and savory meal. whether it be steak or seafood, you have found the spot. This luxurious restaurant has the atmosphere for a real romantic evening mixed with scrumptious food that will please your palate. Open Mon to Fri 11 a.m. to 10 p.m. and Sat noon to 11 p.m. $–$$

Indian Oven. 130 N. Main St.; (435) 787-1757; www.indianovenutah.com. As you walk in, you can feel the atmosphere change: smells from India, music, Indian performances on the TV while you wait (but it never seems to be too long), and, of course, the food that can take you miles away . . . almost as though you are in India. We always feel welcome and pampered by those who run this restaurant. It is not just a meal, it's an experience. Open Mon to Sat 11 a.m. to 10 p.m. $

Iron Gate Grill. Historic Downtown Logan; 155 North Church St.; (435) 752-5260; www .irongategrill.com. After a long awaited move, the Iron Gate Grill is located in the center of Logan in a beautiful old building that they have renovated. This new restaurant has a very eclectic and metropolitan feel. There is wide range of assorted cuisine that will taunt your taste buds until you are finally able to eat. You will not be disappointed! Open Mon through

Thurs 11 a.m. to 9 p.m., Fri 11 a.m. to 10 p.m., Sat 10 a.m. to 10 p.m., and Sun 10 a.m. to 2 p.m. $

Le Nonne Ristorante. 129 N. 100 East; (435) 752-9577; www.lenonne.com. *"Questo è il magnifico"* translates to "This is magnificent!" If you want the real culinary and dining experience that you would have in Italy, visit Le Nonne. One of the owners, chef Pier Micheli, was born and raised in Forte dei Marmi, in northern Italy on the Tuscan coast, where marble has been mined for centuries and where Michelangelo chose the marble for many of his masterpieces. As a young boy, Pier Antonio Micheli learned traditional northern Italian cooking from both his mother and grandmother. You will not be disappointed as you breathe in the smells of basil, garlic, tomatoes, and fresh bread—then taste the authentic Tuscan specialties that will burst with flavor. The olive dip that is served with each meal will leave you begging for the recipe as will many other dishes. You will find that Le Nonne is a very romantic, old renovated house that has the feeling of simple elegance, surrounded by a stunning yard where you can enjoy the luxury of sitting out on the patio, weather permitting. Le Nonne adds to your dining experience by offering free live entertainment most evenings. Check their website for details. Open for lunch Thurs through Fri 11:30 a.m. to 2:30 p.m. and dinner Mon through Sat 5:30 to 9:30 p.m. $–$$

where to stay

Anniversary Inn. 169 E. Center St.; (435) 752-3443; www.anniversaryinn.com. If you are looking for a room with "adventure," book a night at the Anniversary Inn in the heart of historic downtown Logan. They have 33 luxury suites that are designed around specific themes that can liven up and diversify your every visit. The following amenities are included: warm fresh-baked cookies at check-in, a bottle of iced sparkling cider and 2 pieces of delicious cheesecake in your suite upon arrival, freshly baked breakfast delivered to your suite each morning, jetted tubs, big screen TVs and DVDs. You can take a tour of their suites daily from 1 to 3 p.m. Limit to 2 adults per suite and no pets. $–$$$$

Holiday Inn Express & Suites. 2235 N. Main St.; (435) 752-3444 or (800) HOLIDAY; www .hiexpress.com/logan-ut. With a breathtaking view of the Wasatch Mountains, you can sit and enjoy your complimentary hot breakfast buffet, go for a swim, or work out. The accommodations are luxurious and they offer a huge range of amenities. $–$$

Seasons at the Riter Mansion. 168 N. 100 East; (435) 752-7727 or (800) 478-7459; www.theritermansion.com. This bed-and-breakfast is not only for those looking for a romantic getaway; it is also a great place for an executive retreat. Every room is elegantly decorated and has a whirlpool and fireplace. Included is a full breakfast—no cooking required! The Seasons at the Riter Mansion is located in historic downtown Logan, close to shopping, entertainment, and restaurants. They also do not allow pets. Sorry, "Cupcake." $–$$

Springhill Suites by Marriott. 635 S. 80 East; (435) 750-5180; www.loganspringhillsuites
.com. Everyone likes to holiday at a Marriott. The Springhill Suites has a great blend of style
and hospitality. Close by you will find a few restaurants and a day spa. You can take in the
beautiful surroundings of the hotel along the Logan River. $–$$

northeast

day trip 01

northeast

romance at 9,000 feet:
huntsville, snowbasin resort

On the banks of the picturesque Pineview Reservoir, Huntsville is one of only three small communities in what is known as Ogden Valley. During the summer most of the activities surround the reservoir, which is used for fishing, waterskiing, and boating. Horse-drawn buggies are available for hire in the town square. Despite the short growing season of this high-altitude valley, you will find plenty of fresh local fruits and vegetables at the market. During the winter it is transformed into something you might find in a Norman Rockwell painting. The town square is flooded for ice skating and there are sleighs for hire. Located northeast of Salt Lake City, this sleepy valley is rich in Utah pioneer history, from the markers of the Daughters of the Utah Pioneers to the David O. McKay home, which is available for tours and is on the Utah Historic Register.

getting there

To Huntsville: Travel north on I-15 and take exit 324 onto US 89. Travel north to the I-84 interchange and merge eastbound toward Morgan. From I-84 take exit 92. Continue east on Old Highway and turn left on UT 167 (Trappers Loop Road). Drive 9.5 miles and turn right onto UT 39 (East 900 South) and travel 1.8 miles to Huntsville.

To Snowbasin: Take I-15 northbound and exit to northbound US 89 (exit 324). Merge to I-84 eastbound and exit at Mountain Green (exit 92). Continue east on Old Highway and turn left on SR 167 heading north (just east of the Sinclair station). Turn left on SR 226 heading west and proceed approximately 3 miles to Snowbasin.

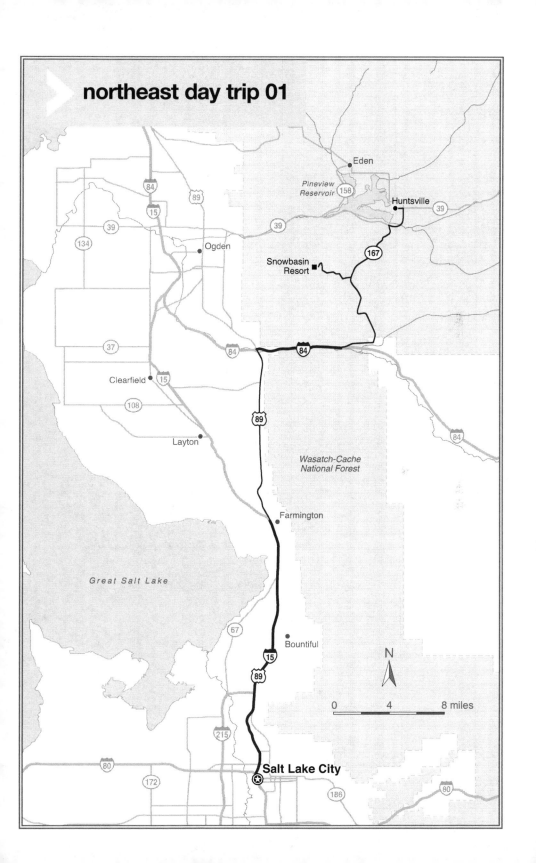

northeast day trip 01

where to go

Snowbasin Resort. Snowbasin became world famous when it hosted the men's and women's downhill and super-G during the 2002 Winter Olympics. Like most ski resorts in Utah, it provides much more than skiing. It has become an all-year, all-weather destination and is one you will note with its own unique style.

Hiking and mountain biking are just a few of the activities available during the non-ski season. Incredible views await those who crest the ridge and look down to the valley below. Begin at the **Grizzly Center** to obtain necessary trail maps, and then take the scenic gondola ride for the best and easiest access to begin your adventure to what might seem to be the top of the world. There are nearly 50 miles of mountain biking trails, from the more moderate family rides for the novice to the incredible uphill climbs and challenging downhill switchbacks for the "gear head." Once again, start at the Grizzly Center, which is just off the Main Plaza, and they can provide you with maps, a shuttle schedule, and even rentals.

Let the kids play! The most difficult dilemma you will have will be deciding which activity to do. The best way to solve this is to plan several trips back to this beautiful area so you can do them all. You might like the group hikes and nature art, flower planting, and tribal mask making, or maybe you will try your hand at the newest mountain sports of disc golf and geocaching. No matter what you choose, you and your kids will be in heaven. All these activities include picnics (with ice-cream sundaes) and free youth gondola tickets. Parents are free (but you need to bring your own lunch). If you want more information about times and availability, or to schedule your day, contact **Children's Mountain Adventure** at (801) 620-1111.

Forget the clubs and play golf! A unique new twist to an old game, disc golf is a challenging sport using the unusual terrain of the mountains for hazards. Snowbasin offers a 9-hole course with no green fees. Challenge your friends or make new ones on the course. Everyone in the family will enjoy the fun and excitement, and—who knows—maybe someone in your family will be the next Jack Nicklaus of disc golf.

Once the day is done and the fun is over (or maybe you skipped the day and just need an incredible night out full of romance), you need look no further than **Needles Lodge** atop Snowbasin for a dining experience like no other. Begin the evening with a romantic gondola ride up to the restaurant. During the summer months, feast on a gourmet buffet with selections to please any palate. The buffet rotates a different theme throughout the month. During the winter, Needles presents a whole new culinary encounter. Here you will order directly from the cook and watch him create your meal right before your eyes. Smell the flavors as your meal cooks, creating a mouthwatering delight even before your first bite is taken. Make sure you have reservations. And don't forget the ride back down, which is priceless!

where to shop

The Eden General Store. 5510 E. 2200 North, Eden; (801) 745-2400. This old-time western store has a little bit of everything.

where to eat

Chris'. 7345 E. 900 South, Huntsville; (801) 745-3542. Open daily 8 a.m. to 10 p.m. This is a great little burger place. Very rustic, with a local flair, there is always a fire on the hearth in the winter with good old home cookin'. $

Gray Cliff Lodge. 508 Ogden Canyon, Ogden; (801) 392-6775; www.grayclifflodge.com. Known for its southern-style fried chicken and dinner rolls covered in cinnamon, this cozy lodge is a wonderful place to stop for a bite to eat. Open Tues through Sat to 10 p.m., Sun brunch (all you can eat) 10 a.m. to 2 p.m., Sun dinner 3 to 8 p.m.; closed Mon. They can make special arrangements for group dinning with additional hours. $$

Needles Lodge. Atop Snowbasin Resort; gondola ride required; (801) 620-1021; www .snowbasin.com/dining/needles. Call for reservations, Open in summer Sat 5:30 to 9 p.m., Sun brunch (summer only) from 10 a.m. to 2 p.m. Winter: Sat only, 5:30 to 9 p.m. Call as times will change from year to year. At nearly 9,000 feet, Needles Lodge is an uncommon restaurant at a distinct location. Enjoy a unique blend of Austrian specialties as well as additional dishes you may be more familiar with. The selection ranges from bratwurst with sauerkraut and *pommes frites* to prime rib, garlic mashed potatoes, mahimahi, and shrimp cocktails. Wonderful and inviting salads are available for those with a lighter palate. Take care that you leave plenty of room for a few selections from the dessert table. The menu varies, so check the website. Perhaps the most romantic part of the evening is the gondola ride back down the mountain. There is something about hanging in midair with nothing but stars surrounding you and that special someone to cozy up to that just says love. $$–$$$

Texas Pride Barbecue. 235 S. 7400 East, Huntsville; (801) 745-2745. Open Mon, Tues, and Thurs 11 a.m. to 8 p.m., Fri and Sat 11 a.m. to 9 p.m. Located in the historical Huntsville Square, you won't find a setting or Texas-style barbecue like this anywhere else in the mountains. Whether you like it slow-smoked or dry-rubbed you will love the flavor and this fun, relaxed dining atmosphere. $

where to stay

Jackson Fork Inn. 7345 E. 900 South, Huntsville; (801) 745-0051. Originally a historic dairy barn, Jackson Fork is now a beautifully converted rustic inn with rooms that capture the imagination. A self-serve complimentary continental breakfast is included. $$–$$$

Snowberry Inn. 1315 N. Hwy. 158, Eden; (801) 745-2634, (888) 746-2634; www.snow berryinn.com. There is nothing better than waking up in the morning to the smell of an incredible breakfast. At the Snowberry Inn, you don't get your typical continental breakfast but rather a buffet that satisfies the senses and gets you ready for the busy day ahead. Top that with wonderful hosts, fantastic rooms, and an outdoor hot tub and you'll be relaxed in every way. The tranquil lake is just across the street and the views are amazing. $$–$$$

day trip 02

northeast

hooves & skis:
logan canyon, beaver mountain,
logan river

logan canyon

Logan Canyon is one of the most beautiful canyons in Utah and is a nature lover's paradise. Scenic hiking trails and picturesque drives are just the beginning in this robust northeastern destination. Both experienced spelunkers and less daring explorers will discover the depth of the many caves. Bring your rock climbing shoes and your hiking boots to probe the many trails and cliff faces amongst the beautiful pines and aspen groves.

The entire canyon is set alongside the Logan River, one of the premier trout fishing streams in Utah. Several dams were created for power and to help divert much needed water to the valley below. These are prime areas to fish or just have a picnic on your way to one of the many destinations that await you.

getting there

From Salt Lake City, drive north about 55 miles on I-15 to exit 362, Brigham City 1100 South. Turn right onto US 91/US 89 and continue on US 91/US 89 26 miles, following the signs to Logan. In the city of Logan, turn right on 400 North (US 89) and drive past the university and into Logan Canyon. Enter the canyon just as you pass over the river for the first time. (Follow the directions for each of the listed places to go or look for the signs.)

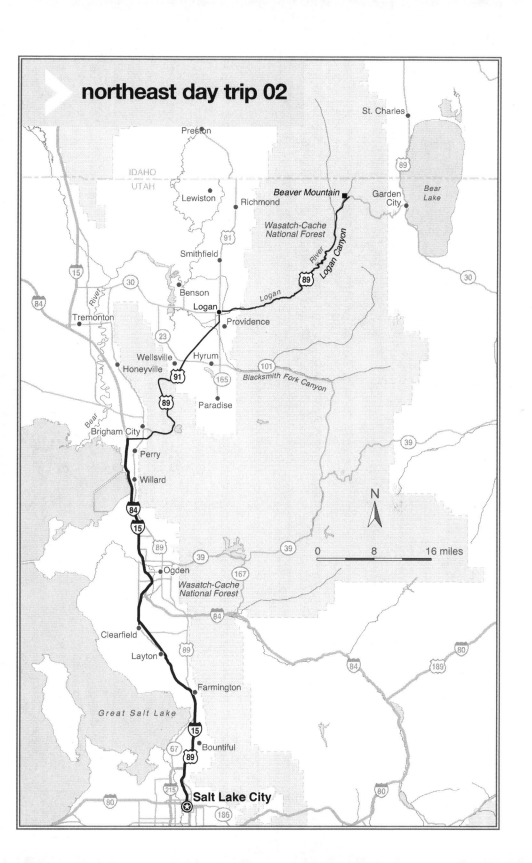

northeast day trip 02

where to go

Stokes Nature Center. From Logan, take US 89 east for approximately 1 mile; (435) 755-3239; www.logannature.org. Located just past the entrance of the canyon near the Logan River. Get ready for exploration and learning. Designed for all ages, Stokes Nature Center is a hands-on house and organization championing the understanding, appreciation, and stewardship of the natural world. You and your children will marvel at the programs, classes, and exhibits. It is not uncommon to hear black-capped chickadees singing, or to see the abundance of canyon wildlife through the center's windows.

Additional animal "friends" reside inside the center. Participate in scheduled programming, or just drop by—Stokes is a great destination by itself, or as a way station on your trek down River Trail. Note that the Stokes Nature Center is a little tricky to find if you don't know where to look. You will find parking on the north side of the road, and you will walk across the road to the River Trail that leads to the center. (Parents keep an eye on the kids as you cross the road.)

Logan Canyon National Scenic Byway. (435) 755-1890; www.logancanyon.com. The Logan Canyon National Scenic Byway offers plenty of extreme natural beauty, varying recreational opportunities, and amazing tales to satisfy even the most demanding adventurer. You can travel this byway by foot, bicycle, or car. Whichever you choose, you'll have a truly wonderful story to share. It will take you through colorful and enchanting patches of wildflowers, bushes, and trees as you wind around steep cliffs of limestone and along picturesque streams bursting with trout. This stretch of US 89 is located approximately 90 miles north of Salt Lake City and runs from the city of Logan to the clear turquoise waters of Bear Lake.

Just before entering Logan Canyon, you will find the grassy park that marks the first of three dams. There wasn't too much imagination or even inspiration in the naming of the dams; they were simply numbered, with the first being the closest to Logan. On a beautiful sunny day, you will find the banks of First Dam alive with activity: people sunbathing, playing volleyball, and picnicking. Being so close to Utah State University, there will of course be plenty of college students who are either catching those last few days of sunshine before winter sets in, or relishing the warm spring afternoons you can only find in Logan Canyon after the snow melts away. Open your picnic basket and if you are willing to share your food, you will make some new friends with the local geese and ducks. There are also plenty of spots to plant your fishing pole in hopes of catching one of the many fish that are stocked here.

Wind Caves. Located 5.2 miles up Logan Canyon, just off US 89, at mile marker 379. This 2-mile trail leads you to natural caves that have been formed by wind and water erosion over thousands of years. An informative kiosk at the head of the trail provides information about the hike, the Wind Caves themselves, the renowned Townsend's big-eared bat, and the incredible variety of rare plants in the canyon. This self-guided hike will take your breath away, literally. It does have a notable incline, approximately 1,000 feet above the canyon floor, but is suitable for all hiking abilities if you go at your own pace. At a certain point along the trail, it will split; if you're heading for the caves, make sure you stay to the left. Hikers are also warned not to cut through the switchbacks on this particular trail to help maintain the delicate nature of the steep slope, and for safety. It is best to hike in the early morning hours during the hot summer months and make sure you bring plenty of water. Once you reach the caves, you'll be able to enjoy a clear view of the "China Wall." This unique formation was created by the incredible force of the winds that are prevalent around the majority of this midsection of the canyon. A delicate arch is also a popular point of interest. If you haven't already taken hundreds of pictures at this point, you will here.

Logan River. As you enter Logan Canyon, you can't help but notice the gorgeous river that seems to dance with the road as it meanders back and forth. Driving along its banks you will notice many people below attempting to catch that ever-elusive dinner. The wonderful thing you will find about this beautiful river is that it is very accessible. Along your 30-mile journey you will find many turnouts with numerous picnicking and camping areas.

What would it be like to catch a 37¾-pound brown trout? Is it just a fisherman's dream or the proverbial fish tale? Not only is this a prize fishing spot for many in the northern Utah area, it is also one of the best blue-ribbon streams in the Intermountain Region. A monster brown trout was caught at First Dam many years ago. Although a fish of that size is unlikely today, you never know, and fantastic fishing for both the sportsman and the novice is definitely the catch of the day. Brown and rainbow trout are the most commonly found fish in the lower river and in First, Second, and Third Dams. These impounds are stocked, so success can be enjoyed by all. Limits are enforced too, so make sure to get information from Fish and Game when getting your permit.

It is important to keep in mind that this beautiful river becomes an intense torrent from late May through most of June because of snow runoff. Fishing is nearly impossible during this time, but check with the local sports suppliers in Logan for conditions—and which fly is best to use.

Tony Grove. Drive farther in Logan Canyon on US 89, about 19 miles out of Logan, turn left heading west at the sign for the Tony Grove Recreation Area (milepost 393.8), and then continue 7 miles to the campground; (435) 245-6521. Here you will find several trails, including the very easy path that circles the lake. Besides the lake trail there are many others that all begin at the lake and will take you deep into the Mt. Naomi Wilderness area or up to the majestic White Pine Lake. All the trails have excellent views of the surrounding area and are a great opportunity to see the abundance of wildflowers, which are in full bloom from July through early Aug. This place is also teeming with wildlife. Moose, elk, and deer are among the larger animals that make this area their home.

Keep in mind that the lake is over 8,000 feet above sea level, and due to this elevation and the long shadows of the surrounding mountains, it is usually still snow and ice bound through most of June. Early summer here is like a lovely spring day in the valley below.

The Tony Grove campground is located above the lake on a beautiful mountainside. This isn't a spot where you can just show up and camp, however. You must make reservations at least 7 days before your arrival date. Reservations can be made for camping mid-Apr through mid-Oct and are available up to 6 months in advance. Please bring your own trash bags and drinking water. Remember that when camping in Apr, May, or early June, you may encounter some cold nights—and the occasional snowmobiler during the day who is trying to get the most out of every last flake of snow. The 3-mile hike to the west of the lake leads hikers to the summit of Mount Naomi. This nearly 10,000-foot peak is the highest and most rugged of the Bear River Mountain Range. White Pine, a small glacial lake, is located on Mount Naomi and is not to be missed. White Pine is about a 2-mile hike from Tony Grove and the only way to reach it is by hiking, backpacking, or horse packing.

Beaver Mountain Ski Resort. 40000 E. US 89, (located 27 miles east of Logan), Garden City; (435) 753-4822; www.skithebeav.com. Experience firsthand the passion that Luella and Harold Seeholzer had for the outdoors. Their desire to make a fun recreational place for their young family to spend time together during the winter months was achieved when they built this magnificent playground. No one could have predicted that this family's vision would turn out to be one of northern Utah's major landmarks and one of the finest small ski areas in Northern Utah. Some even consider this family-owned resort to be one of Utah's best-kept secrets. So, shhhhhh! Enjoy, but don't tell anyone.

The mountain started with just a simple towrope in the late 1940s and has continued to grow ever since. In 1970 one of the favorite lifts was open to the public. "Harry's Dream," as the lift was named, fulfilled one of Harold's greatest desires, which was to have a double chairlift that could take guests from the very bottom to the very top of Beaver Mountain. It is a 4,600-foot double chairlift with 137 chairs, which can accommodate 900 people per hour. This lift added nearly 50 acres of new ski runs on the powder snow that Utah is famous for. In total, there are nearly 664 accessible acres, with runs ranging from gentle green (beginner runs) to challenging black-diamond trails. The well-maintained slopes are situated perfectly for northeastern sun exposure and avalanche-free conditions. This versatile mountain is also an excellent spot for other winter activities such as cross-country skiing and snowmobiling. The Beav's winter season usually runs from Dec to Mar, ending with the "Big Air" contest. Big Air is a fun yet teeth-chattering set of events that range from locals competing in a ski jump to a pond-skimming event. This entertaining affair will leave you cheering for participants and glad that you're wise enough to stay warm and dry!

Beaver Mountain is also a great summer destination. Families can rent the main lodge on the mountain or stay in the RV park or campground. Activities include fishing, hiking, horseback riding, and boating. It is a truly magnificent location to get away to for a day—or maybe two or three. Because of its close proximity to Logan, and only minutes away from beautiful Bear Lake, it truly is a day trip that is also a little slice of heaven!

Beaver Creek Lodge. Logan Canyon, US 89 (27 miles east of Logan); (800) 946-4485; bcl@cut.net. This rustic, 11-bedroom lodge is an easy and scenic drive through Logan Canyon. Though you may think of it more as a place to stay a night or two, it is also a wonderful day trip destination. The rolling hills surrounding the lodge rank among the top 15 snowmobiling places in the West, with hundreds of miles of groomed trails and off-trail riding. Children can enjoy beginner trails, while mothers or fathers can explore the more difficult mountain climbing rides, if they dare.

Snowmobile rentals and guided tours are available to those who wish to enjoy a day of sunlight shining on the soft white snow, without the pressure of preplanning all the mountain trails. One tour is an 80-mile round trip trail that passes through "The Sinks" and leads to Hardware Ranch. Once there, you are invited to take a break and enjoy the Hardware Ranch visitor center or participate in a sleigh ride through a massive elk herd. Another favorite guided tour takes you into the neighboring state of Idaho, where free time is available to carve your sled into the deep snow before heading down to Bear Lake. (Take time to stop in Garden City and sip a steaming cup of hot chocolate and eat a pile of crispy fries.) Intermediate rides will take you to altitudes of over 9,700 feet. At this height individuals will view the world—well, almost—because from here you can see the Grand Tetons of Wyoming to the north and the Uinta Mountains of Utah to the south. On this tour you can take a thrilling ride though a natural mountain luge, which the Beaver Creek owners call the "pig trough." Play for hours on steep draws and high banks in what will surely be a highlight of your famous guided tour. Even for the truly advanced snowmobiler, a guide is recommended. Your experienced guide knows where to find the best extreme play areas with the deepest powder and steepest mountains.

Beaver Creek Lodge isn't just a winter lover's dream. Fun in the sun is also available. Horseback riding is also a popular activity. Trails of varying lengths and difficulty are available so riders can enjoy the beautiful Cache National Forest scenery. Oh, to indulge in horseback tours in the fall! Feeling like you are riding in a watercolor painting is not an understatement. The hues of gold, red, and rust are never ending and truly breathtaking!

where to stay

Beaver Creek Lodge. Logan Canyon, US 89 (27 miles east of Logan); (800) 946-4485; bcl@cut.net. The rolling hills of Logan Canyon have the Beaver Creek Lodge nestled among this pastoral setting. This lodge has 11 guest rooms to satisfy your need for serenity and solitude. You can hike, snowmobile, ATV, and more, just outside your bedroom door. They do have package deals that include snowmobile rentals, breakfast, and some dinners. Check their website for availability and details. $$$

day trip 03

northeast

spelunking & splashing
rich county, bear lake, garden city,
and st. charles (idaho)

rich county

Rich just happened to be the last name of Charles Rich, who led the first settlement here in 1863, but it is also a fitting name for this little piece of paradise, as it is rich in so many ways.

Bear Lake takes diverse to the extreme, offering speed boating, sailing, waterskiing, riding a Jet Ski, rafting, kayaking, fishing, ATVing, snowmobiling, cross-country skiing, ice fishing, golfing, bird watching, etc. For the winter outdoor enthusiasts, the Bear Lake region boasts some of the best snowmobiling in the western US according to both riders and snowmobile magazines. For a more quiet, subdued winter spot, relax, unwind, and enjoy the art of ice fishing on the beautiful, frozen Bear Lake.

If you want to see the "Caribbean of the Rockies" you need go no farther than Bear Lake. Gazing at the water's most beautiful turquoise-blue color, you might just forget that you are in Utah and not some far off exotic location.

getting there

From Salt Lake City, drive north about 55 miles on I-15 to exit 362, Brigham City 1100 South. Turn right onto US 91/US 89 and continue on US 91/US 89 26 miles; follow the signs to Logan. In the city of Logan, turn right on 400 North (US 89) and drive past the university and into Logan Canyon. Follow US 89 to the summit and down the other side. US 89 will take you to the main crossroads in Garden City and Bear Lake itself.

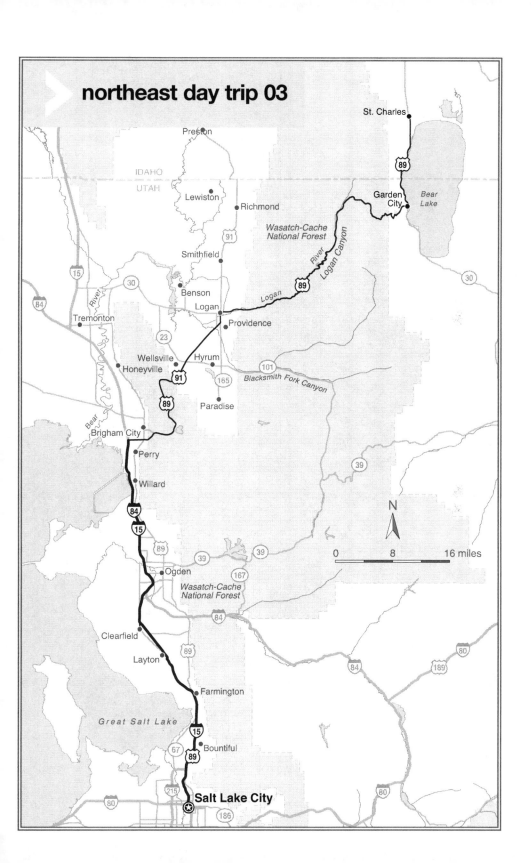

northeast day trip 03

where to go

Bear Lake, of course! 1030 N. Bear Lake Blvd., Garden City; (435) 946-3343. www .bearlake.org. This huge lake was once part of Lake Bonneville, which covered much of the region. The remnants of this massive inland sea are of course the Great Salt Lake, and, farther north, the large freshwater counterpart, Bear Lake.

There are 3 main recreation areas on the Utah side of the lake. The **east beach** or **shoreline** is a great location for camping and fishing. **Rendezvous Beach** on the **south shore** is best for boating, riding a Jet Ski, and fun. (This location was the site where the fur trappers and Indians would trade their goods.) The west shore has limited access and is where the main marina is located. Just a few blocks south of the main intersection in **Garden City** is the **city park.** This is a great place for easy access to the west shore. Park your car and follow the boardwalks down to the beach. Shallow pools make an ideal place for both young and old to play and build sand castles. The one thing you will need to know about Bear Lake is that there are very few places to hide from the warm summer sun. Bring your own shade and plenty of sunblock.

No matter the season, Bear Lake is beautiful and has plenty of activities. Jet Ski, fish for huge mackinaw or cutthroat trout, or sail off into the sunset. If you don't have your own person watercraft, there are several rental locations on the lake. **Bear Lake Sails** is located at 2141 S. Bear Lake Blvd., Garden City; (435) 946-8600 or (866) 867-5912. They have everything you need for a fun, safe day on the more than 160 square miles of this turquoise-blue water.

If you love the cold, Bear Lake is one of the best ice-fishing locations in the world. Here 4 species of fish are found that cannot be found anywhere else in the world. Best known of these is the Bonneville cisco. Spawning in early Jan, ciscoes are easily dip-netted through the ice near the east shore and make excellent bait fish for the larger lake trout. Bore a hole, pull up a seat, and watch what is known as Swedish TV. It is amazing how warm it will get on the ice at near zero degrees when the sun is shining brightly on you.

Minnetonka Cave. From Garden City, Utah, drive 12.3 miles north just past St. Charles, Idaho. Turn west onto St. Charles Canyon Road, and then drive 10 miles to the parking lot near the cave entrance; (435) 245-4422; www.bearlake.org/cavexplore.html. Located in the Caribou National Forest, Minnetonka Cave is a place where you will marvel at the many natural wonders. The cave was accidentally found by Edward Arnell in the summer of 1906 or 1907. While looking for meat for his evening meal, Arnell felt a cool breeze coming from the rock face. He searched the area and discovered a very small cave opening. Return-ing the next day, he explored deeper into the cave with a few other people. Even after the discovery, very little interest was shown until 1938 when the government undertook the first real development of the cave. Closed during the war years, Minnetonka reopened in 1949 and was managed by various organizations until 1995, when concessionaires contracted with the park service to manage the cave operations.

Minnetonka Cave has 9 rooms of wondrous stalagmites, stalactites, and travertine, which were part of the original discovery in the early 1900s. The most stunning of these is called the **Bride,** known for its lacy appearance. As you are led deeper into the cave on a 90-minute, ½-mile guided tour, you will traverse your way up and down windy passages in awe. Make sure you bring your jacket as the cave stays a cool 40 degrees year-round.

Open daily from June to Labor Day, 10 a.m. to 5:30 p.m. Don't arrive too close to closing time since they are often so busy that your chances of finding an hour that's not booked are slim. Your best bet is to come early in the day or make reservations. Tour fee: adults $7, children $5.

Pickleville Playhouse. 2049 S. Bear Lake Blvd., Garden City; (435) 946-2918; www .picklevilleplayhouse.com. Get ready for the night of your life. Pickleville Playhouse will give you the most unique live theater experience with incredible productions and hilarious melodramas that will please any crowd. You will be laughing the entire night. This friendly theater is fun for all ages and is right across the street from Bear Lake on the south side. Combine the play with their Famous Western Cookout for an evening you will never forget. Pickleville is open year-round and is known for the Christmas performances. A day at the beach or on the Day Rides, dinner, and a performance in the evening . . . could life really get any better than this?

Bear Lake Day Rides. Bear Lake/Garden City (KOA); 485 N. Bear Lake Rd., Garden City; (435) 946-3454. Check out this cute town while riding any one of the myriad bicycles avail-able to rent from Bear Lake Day Rides. Shops and scenic pathways are really in very close proximity to each other. Take off on a bicycle built for 2—or 3, or 4, or more—and in a short few hours you will have a few new family adventures to talk about. They have train bikes with 1 or 2 trailers, tricycles, small and large surreys, quadricycles, banana bikes, and, last but not least, mountain bikes. The train bikes with trailers are great for families—you are always together and never have to wait for anyone to catch up. Call ahead for reservations because these guys are always busy. They are also conveniently located next to the KOA campground just south of Garden City

Bear Lake Hot Springs. 7 miles east of St. Charles, Idaho; (208) 945-4545; www.bear lakefun.com/bearlakehotsprings.html. Soak away your troubles in the soothing warm waters of Bear Lake Hot Springs. The springs are located right on the beach at the north-east corner of Bear Lake, on the Idaho side. Not only do they have the calming, hot mineral pools, they also offer Sea-Doo and boat rentals (available on-site at the beach area) and a campground. So here is the plan: Rent a boat and water-ski or wakeboard all morning; then drag your tired old body back to the mineral pools and relax while breathing in the view of the tranquil and beautiful Bear Lake you just conquered.

where to shop

Bear Lake Golf Pro Shop. 2180 S. Country Club Dr., Garden City; (435) 946-8742. If there is anything you need for your golfing adventure, look no further; they have a variety of merchandise and name brands.

Clea's Nifty Gifts. 55 W. Logan Rd., Garden City; (435) 946-8538. This cute little store hosts many different products, including locally made handcrafts and a variety of the good ol' raspberry products that Bear Lake is known for. Open daily from 10 a.m. to 6 p.m., but only during the summer season.

Lighthouse Landing. 10 S. Bear Lake Blvd., Garden City; http://bearlake.com/shop .php?id=lighthouse. This quaint and unique gift shop features home decor, craft items, candles, old-fashioned toys, collectibles, and resort wear. You will find it hard to just "take a quick look," but you will surely be able to find the perfect souvenir or something great for that special someone.

where to eat

Bear Lake Pizza Co. 240 S. Bear Lake Blvd., Garden City; (435) 946-3600. This specialty pizza house has some of the most fantastic pizza you will ever experience. Two of the house specialties are the Chic-Chili Verde and the Chic-Bacon Ranch—you will never want to go back to good ol' pepperoni. They also have an adjoining shop where they sell many Bear Lake homemade items, gifts, and candies, including our favorite, chocolate-covered raspberries! They absolutely melt in your mouth. $

Cafe Sabor. 82 N. Bear Lake Blvd.; Garden City; (435) 946-3297; www.cafesabor.com. "*Olé!*" (which means, "Bravo!") is the first reaction you will have after tempting your taste buds with all the amazing things to eat at this restaurant that touts food from "south of the border." As you start with their well-known salsa, make sure that you save room for the food, as it does not come in small portions. If you are in the mood to sit on their covered outdoor patio, just put in your request. Cafe Sabor is the perfect recipe for your cravings—it has the ideal mix of flavors that complement one another. Check their website for dates of live entertainment. Open Mon through Thurs 11 a.m. to 10 p.m. and Fri and Sat 11 a.m. to 11 p.m. $

Quick and Tasty. 28 N. Bear Lake Blvd., Garden City; (435) 946-2875. Hands down, this is by far the best tasting raspberry shake in the city. Bear Lake is known for its amazing climate for growing raspberries, so naturally they are famous for their raspberry shakes, chocolate-covered raspberries, and many other raspberry delights. Quick and Tasty has loads of other milk shake flavors to choose from but raspberry seems to be most everyone's favorite. $

where to stay

Bear Lake/Garden City KOA. 485 N. Bear Lake Rd., Garden City; (435) 946-3454; www .koa.com/where/ut/44101. This KOA campground offers many options and amenities so that you can explore to your heart's desire. You may stay at an RV site, a tent site, or a beautiful new cabin. Enjoy the swimming pool, ping-pong, pool table, playground, kids' jumping "pillow," miniature golf, bicycle rentals, and much more. While staying there you can also enjoy all the local attractions: fishing, water sports, horseback riding, hiking, and golf. $

Inn at Snow Meadows. 1006 Snow Meadows Dr., Garden City; (435) 512-9974; www .bearlakeutahspecialevents.com. The Inn at Snow Meadows is Bear Lake's largest resort and you will feel bathed in luxury as you stay in one of the "themed" suites. You will have a truly unforgettable visit of elegance and pleasure. They offer custom packages, including an anniversary package that consists of flowers, chocolates, sparkling cider, chilled champagne, a fruit basket, and more. $–$$

east

day trip 01

east

mount olympus made of gold:
park city, deer valley

The 2002 Olympics, in Park City, was said to have been the most successful Winter Olympics ever. During those eventful days, hundreds of thousands of visitors from all over the world came to watch the world's best athletes compete for gold. In the mid-1800s, people flocked to Park City seeking silver. Today, visitors and residents gather for many other reasons.

Park City is an incredible blend of rustic, old, outdoorsy, luxurious, and artistic. When you walk up the main street of Park City, especially at dusk when the lights of the buildings are just beginning to glow and light up the beautiful mountains surrounding the town, you can't help but deeply take in the sights, the smells, and the fresh air. This is why Park City has hosted some of the most elegant film festivals, celebrations, and other events in Utah.

Here comes the powder! Park City is not the only town known for its incredible skiing in this valley; rather, there are 3 uniquely and distinctly different ski areas here. Deer Valley is an original, having revolutionized the ski industry over 3 decades ago. It was the first to provide first-class ski service that could only be found at a 5-star hotel. Deer Valley has the ability to offer everything that will make your trip "memorable." The third ski area is the Canyons. With a bit of a flair for the faster pace of life, it still has an elegance and hint of sophistication all its own.

When looking for the "perfect" vacation, you cannot go wrong with this valley. Whether it be winter or summer, your adventurous spirit will be superbly filled.

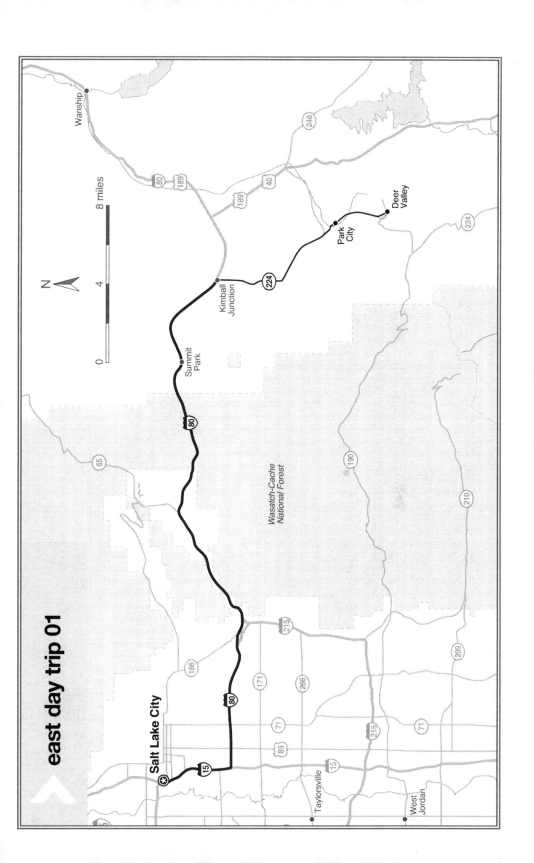

east day trip 01

getting there

Be prepared for the beautiful drive eastbound on I-80 from Salt Lake City to Park City, which is only about 28 miles. Take exit 145 (Kimball Junction) onto UT 224, going south toward Park City.

where to go

Utah Olympic Park. 3419 Olympic Parkway; (435) 658-4200; www.olyparks.com. You can spend the entire day (winter or summer) just watching the phenomenal athletes that come here to train, but there are many other fun activities, if you can pull yourself away:

- Daily guided **tours of Olympic competition sites**. Come see how it would feel to travel to the top of the world's highest-altitude ski jumps and see the fastest bobsled, luge, and skeleton track, and experience where Olympic history was made. During winter training you can watch the athletes ski jump off the K90 and K120 Nordic hills, launching themselves into the air to then float effortlessly, for what seems like an eternity, down the mountain.

- Interactive **Alf Engen Ski Museum.** You will experience and learn all you need to know about Utah's ski history, as well as the more recent history of the 2002 Olympic Winter Games in this interactive museum. Admission is free.

- Public **bobsled rides**. Have you ever wanted to experience 5Gs of force at 80 miles an hour—the equivalent of a drop from a 40-story building in less than a minute? Slide yourself into a 4-person passenger bobsled ride, hold on tight, and don't you dare close your eyes or even blink or you will miss this spine-tingling ride down the entire length of the track. You, along with 3 willing volunteers and an expert, will get to experience what few in the world have ever have—the rush and acceleration of an Olympic athlete on a quest for the gold. You must be 16 years of age or older. The cost is $60 per person but the second ride is only $30.

- **Chairlift ride to the top of K120 Ski Jump.** Feel your heart pound as you look down on the Snyderville Basin from this, the highest-altitude ski jump (7,130 feet), at the K120 starting house. Not only will they take you up on their chairlift, but if you behave, they might even bring you back down—on the chairlift, that is, not the ski jump. Cost: adults $5, seniors and youth $3. Admission is free to get into the Olympic Park to explore and watch athletes train. Open 10 a.m. to 6 p.m., but closed Thanksgiving, Christmas, New Year's, and Easter.

Summer activities at Utah Olympic Park include:

- The **Xtreme Zip,** zip line with a 435-foot vertical drop, $15 to $20 per person.

- The **Quicksilver,** Utah Olympic Park's stainless-steel alpine slide. Solo riders must be 8 years and up. Cost: $15, or $20 when sharing with a child age 3 through 7.

- A summer bobsled ride on **The Comet.**

- Expert-**guided tours.**

- Introductory **sport clinics** offered for all ages and abilities.

- **Freestyle Exhibition Shows** every Sat.

Deer Valley. (800) 424-DEER; www.deervalley.com. Deer Valley will make you feel so pampered you may never want to leave, especially since they offer such a diverse sum of activities for everyone. The top reasons most people come to Deer Valley are the multiple mountains and the greatest snow on Earth. Skiers of all skill levels will find a slope that's just right. If skiing isn't your cup of tea, or if you have had your fill for the day, here are a few of the other activities that might keep you busy (and don't forget they have some wonderful lodging options).

Nastar. (435) 645-6876; www.nastar.com. Open daily from 10 a.m. to 3 p.m. during the winter season. Nastar is the biggest recreational ski race program in the world and is offered at over 120 of the nation's premier resorts.

Summit Meadows Adventures. (800) 424-3337. These snowmobile tours are located on the Garff Ranch, where you can access 7,000 acres of pristine open rolling hills to snow-mobile to your heart's content.

All Seasons Adventures. www.allseasonsadventures.com. All Seasons Adventures is a year-round guided activity service offering amazing outdoor experiences for every season and sport available. They have professional and friendly guides who will take care of every-thing you need. Their summer adventures include ATV tours, trapshooting, fly fishing, rafting and kayaking, and much more. Winter adventures include hot-air ballooning, sleigh rides, heli-skiing, cross-country skiing, dogsledding, snowshoeing, and more.

Park City Mountain Resort. 1310 Lowell Ave.; Park City; (435) 649-8111; www.parkcity mountain.com. Park City Resort is found nestled among the majestic mountains surround-ing historic Main Street. In 2010 Park City Mountain Resort was again ranked the most accessible mountain resort and was among the top 5 ski resorts in North America. With the resort just 40 minutes from Salt Lake City International Airport, you can fly into Salt Lake City in the morning and be on the slopes by lunchtime.

- **Alpine Coaster.** How would you like to ride on Utah's only alpine coaster? Relax on the uphill ascent before beginning the harrowing and fun 1-mile track of loops and curves. Charge is by rider height: Over 54 inches is $20 and under 54 inches is $7, but they do have a combo pass—Alpine Coaster/Alpine Slide Combo for $25.

- **Alpine Slide.** The Alpine Slide at Park City Mountain Resort is one of the longest slides in the world—over 3,000 feet of sheer fun and a few screams. Because you have 4 tracks to choose from, you can experience a different thrill ride every time. The prices vary depending on height, and hours of operation depend on the season. Call for details.

- **ZipRider.** For a real treat, don't forget your ticket for the ZipRider. This will take you through the air for an exhilarating adventure that you will never be able to forget—even if you want to. High above the ground you will enjoy a scenic view of the resort while flying at speeds up to 45 mph. Riders must be between 75 and 275 pounds.

- **Other summer and winter activities include** scenic lift rides, Legacy Launcher, a climbing wall, hiking, horseback riding, Little Miners Park, kids' signature programs, and last but not least, **SKIING!** Open various times and seasons so call for details.

The Canyons Resort. The Canyons Resort is known for its skiing and accommodations. It is embarking on a multiyear recreation plan designed to make it one of the top 4-season destination resorts in North America. There will be 19 lifts plus an 8-passenger gondola, a 6-passenger express, 6 high-speed quads, and more. They offer many choices for adventures all year:

- **Dogsledding.** (435) 615-4848. There is no age limit to experience this "once in a lifetime" adventure. Sail through the snow-covered meadows in a dogsled that is pulled by a team of Siberian huskies.

- **Heli-skiing.** Wasatch Powderbird Guides, (801) 742-2800 or (800) 974-4354; www .powerbird.com. They now offer heli-ski trips into the backcountry from The Canyons Resort. This is not for the faint of heart! This exhilarating experience is for those who want an extreme adventure in skiing the acres of untracked Utah powder. If you are a powderhound, don't think too hard, just call and book your adventure today.

- **Snowmobile tours.** (435) 615-4848. What a great way to see the backcountry, up close and personal, as you wind through the scenic and secluded mountains.

- **Other summer and winter activities include** trapshooting, fly fishing, cross-country skiing, western cookouts, horse-drawn sleigh rides, hiking, fast track, groomer ride-along, guided snowshoe tours, horseback riding, and last but not least, **SKIING!** Open various times and seasons, so call for details.

The Park City Museum. 528 Main St., Park City; (435) 649-7457; www.parkcityhistory .org. The Park City Museum is located in the old 1885 City Hall, where they offer exhibits on mining and skiing history, including an original restored stagecoach. They also have history presentations and a historic walking tour. Not only can you learn about the diverse area and history of Park City, but they offer other tours, some of which might be bit "hair-raising"—Dungeon Party: Night at the Museum.

Park City visitor centers. Kimball Junction, 1862 Olympic Parkway, Park City; (435) 658-9616 or Historic Main Street Visitor Information Center, Park City Museum, 528 Main St.; (435) 649-7457; www.parkcityinfo.com. If you need any additional information, coupons, information on current events, etc., they can help, as well as provide you with brochures and maps. Open every day.

where to shop

Art Galleries. Check out www.parkcityinfo.com (and click on shopping and service, then Art Galleries), as there is a diverse and immense amount of galleries to please all art connoisseurs.

Bunya Bunya. 511 Main St., Park City; (435) 649-1256. This downtown boutique has a funky edge to its merchandise. If you are looking for hip clothes and fashionable trends with many hot brands, you don't want to miss this shop.

Livin' Life. 577 A Main St., Park City; (435) 655-0111; www.livinlifeparkcity.com. Livin' Life offers a variety of specialty items for someone special, for your home, or for you. When you walk in, you will feel as though you have just arrived in the Southwest or Mountain West. They have a big selection of what some would coin as "Park City Style." Ski season hours are 10 a.m. to 9 p.m.; during the rest of the year they're open 11 a.m. to 6 p.m.

Mountain Town Olive Oil Co. 605 Main St., Park City; (435) 649-1400; www.mountain townoliveoil.com. They offer over 20 olive oils, including superior single varietals from Australia, Europe, and California, as well as 2 organic oils. Some of the infused flavored oils are basil, mushroom, garlic, Persian lime, and chipotle. They have almost as many balsamic vinegars, including blueberry, cherry, blackberry ginger, and tangerine. These mouthwatering culinary delights will put a smile on any chef you know—maybe you. Open every day from 10 a.m. to 6 p.m., except on Sat, when hours are noon to 5 p.m.

Rocky Mountain Chocolate Factory. 510 Main St., Park City; (435) 649-0996; www .rmcf.com. If you want to try some of the hippest and tastiest treats your mouth has ever bitten into, you'll find them at—drumroll please—Rocky Mountain Chocolate Factory. You never knew such delectable goodies existed. One of their specialties is the caramel-dipped apple that is like an apple pie. Try some of their handmade fudge, other creative creations of caramel apples, exquisite chocolates, and truffles. Open every day.

Tanger Outlets. 6699 N. Landmark Dr., Park City; (435) 645-7078; www.tangeroutlet .com/parkcity. First you must ask yourself, "How much time do I really have?" At the Tanger Outlet Center you will find over 60 brand-name outlets to shop to your heart's content, such as Carter's, Van Heusen, Polo Ralph Lauren, J. Crew Factory, and so much more. They are open Sun 11 a.m. to 6 p.m. and Mon to Sat 10 a.m. to 9 p.m.

where to eat

According to Utah Office of Tourism, Park City has more chefs per capita than Paris, France. The Park City area has over 100 restaurants, with some of the most incredible food anywhere in the world. You would be hard pressed to find a bad restaurant, but here are a few good ones you may enjoy. Those we have included are mostly in downtown Park City, and our list does not encompass any of the fine dining offered at the resorts.

Bandits Grill and Bar. 440 Main St., Park City; (435) 649-7337; www.banditsbbq.com. Have you ever wished you could have tangled with the likes of Butch Cassidy? At Bandits, it is likely you will only have to wrestle with some of the best barbecue ever. Bandits Grill has repeatedly been voted best barbecue and has become very famous, like some other bandits, throughout Ventura County and Park City. They slowly cook the barbecue ribs in their Texas-style smoker, while other meats are wood grilled or slow roasted. Mmm . . . Is your mouth watering yet? If you want some downright incredible barbecue, Bandits has it. Open every day. $

Bangkok Thai on Main. 605 Main St.; Park City; (866) 649-THAI or (435) 649-THAI; www .bangkokthaionmain.com. Winner of the "Best of State for Asian/Pacific in Fine Dining" award, Bangkok Thai will give you a truly authentic Thai cuisine experience while you dine in casual luxury. Their dishes lack nothing since they are prepared from the freshest and most exotic ingredients. Open for dinner nightly. $$

Cafe Terigo. 424 Main St., Park City; (435) 645-9555; www.cafeterigo.com. Cafe Terigo specializes in cuisine from northern Italy and southern France—the likes of pesto pizza, fresh pastas, seafood, and much more. "Bon appétit." Lunch is served Mon to Sat 11:30 a.m. to 2:30 p.m.; dinner is served Mon, Tues, Fri, and Sat 5:30 to 9:30 p.m. $$

Dolcetti Gelato. 1476 Newpark Blvd., Suite No. IL-E, Park City; (435) 615-6728; www .dolcettigelato.com. If you have been craving the taste of real gelato from Italy, then you need to visit Dolcetti Gelato. This wonderfully cool treat touts only ⅓ the fat of ice cream and they use only the freshest ingredients and seasonal fresh fruit. There is nothing more sinfully luscious and delectable than good gelato, just like that in Italy. Once you find this little gem, you might be visiting every day. There are other delicacies that you might try as well: sweet or savory crepes, and panini sandwiches. Open every day. $

Ghidotti's Italian Restaurant. 6030 N. Market St., Park City; (435) 658-0669; www .ghidottis.com. Your dining experience at Ghidotti's will feel like you have stepped over to Italy, with its ambience, architecture, and some of the most scrumptious cooking you've ever tasted. As you walk past the hostess to your table, notice the incredible butterfly collection. Ghidotti's is a little drive to the south, across the road from the Olympic Park in the Red Stone shopping complex. It is well worth the drive. If you want to stay closer to downtown, they also have an Italian restaurant at the top of Main Street that is also wonderful, called Grappa. Call for more information: (435) 645-0636. Ghidotti's is open daily. Live entertainment with Sunday brunch. $$–$$$

Red Banjo Pizza. 322 Main St., Park City; (435) 649-9901; www.redbanjopizza.com. Red Banjo Pizza is Park City's oldest establishment. Three cheers for them—in 2010 they were awarded first place for the following awards: "Best Pizza Park City," "Best Customer Service," and "Best of the Best." Knowing that, you won't be disappointed, especially if you order the tried-and-true favorite, the Red Banjo Special. They also serve salads, hot subs, and more. Open every day but Thanksgiving—we guess that means you can order up a Christmas pizza, too. $

Windy Ridge Cafe. 1250 Iron Horse Dr., Park City; (435) 647-0880; www.windyridgefoods .com. This trendy restaurant is one of Park City's best-kept secrets. Whether you want something quick for lunch or you'd like to sit down for a relaxing dinner at a restaurant with style, Windy Ridge is a great place to go. They tout one of the city's best bakeries, with everything from pies, fine pastries, and cakes to distinctive desserts. They also have a deli case stocked with fresh salads, sandwiches, and other delicacies for the connoisseur on the go. During the summer season you can enjoy the ambience of Park City from their beautiful patio. $–$$

Yuki Arashi. 586 Main St., Park City; (435) 649-6293; www.yukiarashi.com. Yuki Arashi is an Asian tapas and sushi bar where they offer the freshest seasonal fish flown in from not only the West Coast but also Japan. Their cuisine consists of traditional Japanese sushi, sashimi, tempura, maki, and Asian tapas, which are a contemporary mix of Korean, Japanese, and French flavors. Try one of their specialties, the maki sushi roll. Yuki Arashi will renew your love for sushi! $

Zoom. 660 Main St., Park City; (435) 649-9108; www.zoomparkcity.com. A part of the Sundance Resort restaurant family, Zoom was opened by the actor Robert Redford in 1995. Zoom exudes sophistication in a casual but vibrant atmosphere. The food is prepared individually by the chefs so that you are promised a meal to remember. Just don't "zoom" to get there! $$–$$$

where to stay

Silver Queen Hotel. 632 Main St., Park City; (435) 645-9696; www.silverqueenhotel.com. If you want to be in the heart of downtown Park City, Silver Queen is the prime location. Beautifully decorated luxury suites will make you feel like you moved your home to the base of the mountains. Once you step out the door you will be on Historic Main Street, where you can enjoy the Park City ambience in restaurants, shops, and entertainment. $$$

The Trace. 476 E. Richins Ranch Rd., Wanship; (435) 336-6031; www.thetracebedand breakfast.com. The Trace bed-and-breakfast is just 15 to 20 minutes from Park City and will accommodate all the things you desire in a serene place to play or just do nothing. There is easy access to the ski slopes, downtown, restaurants, fly fishing, and all other outdoor activities. By night you can snuggle up next to a crackling fire or play some pool—just use your imagination! $$

Washington School Inn Bed and Breakfast. 543 Park Ave., Park City; (435) 649-3800; www.washingtonschoolinn.com. Tucked into the beautiful Wasatch Mountains of Park City, the inn is only a half hour away from Salt Lake City, and they will invite you in like long-lost friends. Originally a schoolhouse built in 1889, it was renovated almost 100 years later, in 1984, into the luxury bed-and-breakfast that you see today. Washington School Inn is a great place to let yourself unwind and be rejuvenated. $$

day trip 02

east

soaring with the eagles:
snowbird resort

Snowbird Resort is located in a glacial canyon called Little Cottonwood. The area was first discovered by a soldier who came across some tiny minerals that resulted in a massive industry of mining. This soldier's discovery will go down in history as being one of the largest generators of silver within the Wasatch Mountains, producing more than $3.8 million dollars worth of silver ore. The town at the base of the narrow canyon ended up housing around 8,000 people. There were 138 homes, hotels, boardinghouses, stores, and a railroad. A run of avalanches later destroyed the entire town.

In 1970, after much research, a project was under way to make a ski resort that would be named Snowbird. The visionary, Ted Johnson, and the financial supporter, Richard Bass, hiked into Gad Valley and recognized that the canyon could house a spectacular resort. Richard Bass stated, "My underlying dream for Snowbird is the creation of a year-round resort, which respects and complements the beauty and inspiration of this natural setting—a place dedicated to increasing human understanding through the enhancement of body, mind, and spirit." Since 1971, when Snowbird opened, it has continued to grow and expand. Today the Sunbird Ski and Summer Resort has some of the most luxurious facilities in the world and is conveniently accessible from a major metropolitan city and international airport. The integrity of Snowbird has been maintained throughout the years, and it has received numerous rewards for high environmental stewardship. The base elevation is 8,100 feet, while Snowbird's highest point, Hidden Peak, is 11,000 feet.

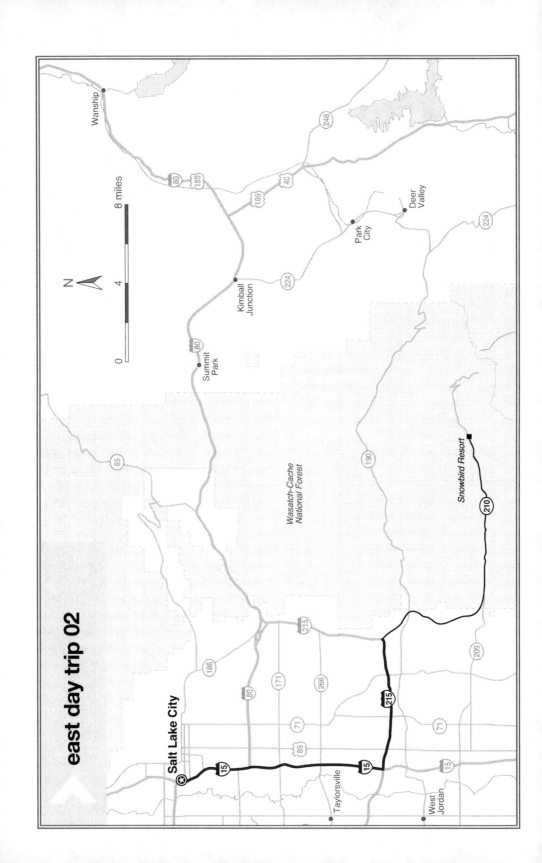

east day trip 02

getting there

From Salt Lake City, travel south on I-15 until you reach the I-215 belt route, exit 298. Merge onto I-215 heading east. Take exit 6 and merge onto UT 190, Cottonwood Road/ Wasatch Boulevard. Continue south on Wasatch Boulevard (UT 210) until you reach Little Cottonwood Canyon Road. Snowbird is about 8 miles up the canyon.

where to go

Snowbird Ski and Summer Resort. UT 210 Little Cottonwood Canyon; (801) 933-2147; www.snowbird.com. The various activities you can take pleasure in include skiing, snow-shoeing, and snowmobiling.

- **Backcountry tours.** www.snowbird.com. Enjoy the solitude of the Wasatch back-country with one of Snowbird's expert guides. Take time to breathe in the air of this magnificent mountain. Three tours are available.

- **Tram ride.** (801) 933-2147; www.snowbird.com. This amazing ride opened in 1971 and allows you to view the Rockies from 11,000 feet! Enjoy a thrilling 1.6-mile ride that climbs 2,900 vertical feet in 10 minutes. Once at the top, called Hidden Peak, you can relax and spend as much time as you wish viewing the slopes.

- **Heli-skiing.** Wasatch Powderbird Guides, headquarters located at the Snowbird Ski Resort; (801) 742-2800 or (800) 974-435; www.snowbird.com. It all began in 1973, when some ski professionals started taking adventurous individuals on heli-ski trips in Utah's regal mountains. You'll be privileged to ski on the unblemished powder of "the greatest snow on earth."

- **Mountain tours.** Snowbird Center Plaza at the orange MOUNTAIN TOUR sign; (801) 933-2147; www.snowbird.com. Get oriented with the mountain and learn many interesting facts about the land you are exploring. Seasonal.

- **Interconnect tours.** (801) 534-1907; www.snowbird.com. You'll be given the exclu-sive opportunity to ski on the outer boundaries of designated ski areas. Experienced guides lead you through the backcountry of 6 different ski resorts. See some of the most beautiful scenery, learn backcountry etiquette, and have the time of your life. Skiers must be 16 and older, and due to the nature of the tour, no snowboards are allowed.

- **Alpine Slide.** (801) 933-227; www.snowbird.com. Snowbird's Alpine Slide will have you screaming with delight as you twist, turn, and go through tunnels. Begin at Snow-bird Entry 4 and finish approximately 1,300 feet below, near the Snowbird Center. Drivers control the speed so all riders can enjoy their slide.

- **Fly fishing.** (801) 933-2147; www.snowbird.com. Fish year-round on the Provo and Weber Rivers. Some of the most experienced guides from the western United States will customize an idyllic fly-fishing experience for you, from still water to streams, winter or summer.

- **Peruvian Gulch to Mineral Basin.** (801) 933-2431. Ride The Peruvian Express 2,400 vertical feet from Snowbird Center to Hidden Peak. Views of the mountainside and wildlife are plentiful. At the top of the chairlift, a 600-foot-long tunnel will lead you to Mineral Basin, where hiking, horse rides, and ATV tours can be provided.

- **ZipRider.** (801) 933-2431; www.snowbird.com. Access the ZipRider by means of the Chickadee lift. Once at the top, climb a 50-foot tower and get harnessed and launched from a deck. Gliding at 30 mph you'll descend 1,000 feet from a suspended cable to Snowbird Center.

- **Guided horseback tours.** (801) 933-2147; www.snowbird.com. High Country Exploring leads guests through Snowbird's backcountry. Begin your adventure by riding Snowbird's Arial Tram to Hidden Peak, 11,000 feet above Snowbird's basin. You will then ride to Mineral Basin on a Polaris Ranger, where you meet up with the wranglers and gentle, trail broke horses. You will see beautiful waterfalls, wildlife, and wildflowers. Seasonal.

where to shop

Cliff Sports. The Cliff Lodge, Level 1, UT 210, Little Cottonwood Canyon; (801) 742-2871; www.snowbird.com/shopping/cliffsports.html. Specializing in fashion, high-tech sportswear, and accessories for young and old, you will find all of your skiing needs in 1 location. You will find superior performance, powder, and demo skis and snowboards. They also offer a state-of-the-art repair shop for anything you might need—even an overnight service is available. Open daily during the ski season from 8 a.m. to 6 p.m.

Kuhl Haus. The Snowbird Center, Level 1, UT 210, Little Cottonwood Canyon; (801) 933-2254; www.snowbird.com/shopping/kuhl.html. Looking for the perfect pair of Oakley sunglasses and goggles, or Dakine gloves and backpacks, or other high-quality fleece, sweaters, or jackets? These great products can be found at the Kuhl Haus. Open daily.

Marco Polo. The Cliff Lodge, Level C, UT 210, Little Cottonwood Canyon; (801) 933-2255; www.snowbird.com/shopping/marcopolo.html. Because Dick Bass, Snowbird's owner, has a passion for international arts and collectibles, these qualities have given Marco Polo a unique distinction. Your shopping experience will allow you to experience the world without ever leaving the shop. In The Gallery they offer international and domestic gifts as well as home decor. They also feature local new artists, handmade Lithuanian blown glass, and an

Oriental carpet collection. Watch out—this store may hold you captive for hours. Open daily from 10 a.m. to 6 p.m.

Wings Snowbird Store. Snowbird Center, Level 1, UT 210, Little Cottonwood Canyon; (801) 933-2193; www.snowbird.com/shopping/wings.html. You will be able to find the official signature logo on any of the store's fashionable apparel, gifts, toys, baseball hats, and much more. These items feature the resort's unique trademark wings. Open 10 a.m. to 6 p.m.

where to eat

The Aerie Restaurant. (801) 933-2160; www.snowbird.com. Located on the 10th floor of the spectacular Cliff Lodge. Relish the ultimate view of mountain scenery from the restaurant's massive 15-foot windows while you dine. Chef Fernando Soberanis will enlighten your taste buds with New American cuisine. The Aerie is the winner of several awards, including Utah's Most Romantic Restaurant. They also have an award-winning wine list, with over 800 selections. $$$

The Atrium Restaurant. (801) 933-2140; www.snowbird.com. Located on Level B of the Cliff Lodge. Perfect for guests who want a relaxed dining atmosphere combined with great food. Patio dining in the summer allows you to enjoy the mountain breeze. Dining is buffet style, so eat up! $ lunch; $$ dinner

The Rendezvous Restaurant. (800) 232-9542; www.snowbird.com. This cafeteria-style restaurant is open daily for lunch in the winter and is closed in the summer. Specialties include a grill with burgers, chicken sandwiches, and a delicious Thai wrap. Try the made-to-order pasta bar, where you pick the pasta and all your favorite toppings. The carousel-shaped salad bar, a real favorite with the locals, offers over 55 items ranging from Middle Eastern hummus to Greek salad, including all the traditional salad bar ingredients. Looking for something to warm you up? Try the smokehouse chili in a bread bowl. They also offer vegetarian menu items such as the garden burger or the grilled veggie sandwich. You are sure to find something to satisfy everyone. It's simple, quick, and delicious—just what you need to refuel and get back out on the mountain. $

The Steak Pit. (801) 933-2260; www.snowbird.com. This is a favorite among the locals and tourists alike. Enjoy bottomless salad, USDA prime steaks, seafood, and vegetarian dishes. Don't forget to leave room for the Steak Pit's signature dessert, mud pie. Yum! $$$

southeast

day trip 01

southeast

where the indian princess lies:
alpine, lehi

It's just a short drive from Salt Lake City, yet Alpine creates the feeling that you are a world away. You soon see why people are flocking to this small community nestled up against the Wasatch Mountains. But don't be fooled by its size or location. Alpine offers scenic views and a wide variety of attractions, from historical family fun to both biking and hiking adventures. Alpine is also the gateway to one of the most magnificent scenic highways, leading you to Timpanogos Cave, and in the summer, the back side of the Sundance Resort. Keep in mind the Alpine Scenic Highway (SR 92) is closed to winter travel.

getting there

From Salt Lake City head south on I-15, 21 miles. Take exit 284 and turn left at the end of the ramp toward Highland/Alpine. Travel 5.5 miles and then turn left on 5300 West, which will turn into Main Street in Alpine. Follow Main Street into the center of town.

where to go

Alpine Art Center. 450 S. Alpine Hwy.; (801) 763-7173; www.alpineartcenter.com. The Alpine Art Center is a 33,000-square-foot building filled with sophistication and culture. It houses an art gallery featuring nationally known and locally produced artwork; it's also a reception center and a bronze art casting facility and gallery. Also on the grounds are gardens with shady paths and a Sculpture Park—10 acres of picturesque sculptures. It's certainly well worth a visit: Mon through Fri 9 a.m. to 5 p.m.

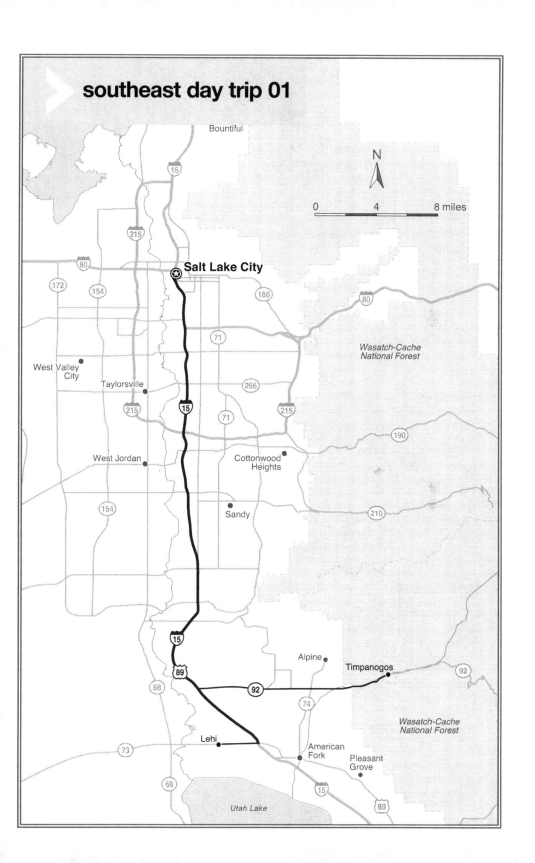

Timpanogos Cave National Monument. On the south side of SR 92; visitor center, (801) 756-5238; headquarters, (801) 756-5239; www.nps.gov/tica. No trip to Utah Valley is complete without a visit to Timpanogos Cave National Monument, located just 5 miles from the town of Alpine and 2.5 miles from the mouth of the mouth of the canyon on SR 92 (American Fork Canyon Road/Alpine Scenic Highway). This naturally formed cave system consists of 3 caves, all well known for the abundant helictites and anthodite crystal formations. The rich coloration and formations are as unique as the legend of the cave itself. The displays in their fault-controlled passages, the breathtaking mountainous surroundings, and of course the unique cave history will be well worth the trek to this natural wonder. Don't forget to bring your hiking shoes because the cave is only reachable by hiking 1.5 miles, which includes 1,100 feet of elevation gain above the canyon floor. The hike may be a little strenuous, but the views along the way and the scene awaiting you at the cave's entrance make it all worthwhile.

Once inside, the exploration begins on a ¾-mile ranger-led tour deep into the cave. Keep in mind that the mountain you are inside has a legend. It is believed that the Indian princess Ucanogas climbed the mountain to wait for the return of her warrior, Timpanac, who was to claim her hand forever. When Timpanac was killed trying to reach her, Ucanogas lay down upon the mountain to be united with him for eternity; hence the combined name of Timpanogos. It was told that Ucanogas's heart would be kept inside the mountain for safekeeping. During your tour you will see a formation perfectly located and perfectly shaped as the heart of Ucanogas.

Cave tours are available throughout the day during the summer. Operating hours: May through Labor Day, 7 a.m. to 5:30 p.m. The first hike inside the cave is at 7:30 a.m. and the last hike at 4:30 p.m. Arrive as early as you can, though, because they take only so many per tour and if you get there right at 4:30, expecting to get in that tour, you will most likely be left behind.

where to eat

Dimitri's Pizzeria. 412 S. Main St., Alpine; (801) 763-1090; www.dimitrispizzeria.com. Dimitri's feels like an old-fashioned sit-down pizzeria. It's a great place for family and friends to get some of the best pizza around, perhaps even in Utah. If you're looking for signature pizzas that aren't run-of-the-mill ordinary, check out the Alfredo with Artichoke Hearts pizza. Here you can sit back and enjoy the relaxed atmosphere as you watch your pizza being made from scratch—and they still hand toss your dough. $

Kneaders Bakery & Cafe. 1384 E. SR 92 (Highland Highway), Lehi; (801)768-9977; www.kneadersbakery.com. Walk in and smell the aroma of fresh-baked bread. This isn't just anyone's bread; this is bread made for the kings of Europe—we're sure of it. There really isn't anything you won't love here, from the pastries to the unique sandwiches and soups. This place is the essence of yummy. $

day trip 02

southeast

where stars touch the ground:
sundance

If you have ever taken the long way home just to escape the noise of the world, to get the feeling you have entered into your own special place, where the cares of the world have no effect on you, you have driven to Sundance. The real drive to Sundance is alone worth the trip, but as you pull up and see it for the first or even the 100th time, it takes your breath away. "Beautiful" cannot begin to describe the 5,000 acres of protected wilderness. Robert Redford has truly created something special here. This is a place where art and nature don't collide—they meld into one another so perfectly that you don't know where one ends and the other begins. All of the activities here are designed to place you in the middle, to create a world of art with you as part of the subject. Whether it is carving your way down the slopes in the winter or watching a summer play on the outdoor stage, take the opportunity to immerse yourself in the world of Sundance.

getting there

Travel south on I-15 toward Provo. Take exit 272 (which is 800 North in Orem, or UT 52) and turn left, traveling to the east. Travel through Orem on 800 North/UT 52 to the mouth of the canyon. Stay in the left lane, which will drop onto US 189. Continue up the canyon approximately 7 miles to Scenic Route 92, which is the first left after the tunnel. Continue an additional 2 miles up the canyon. Sundance is on the left.

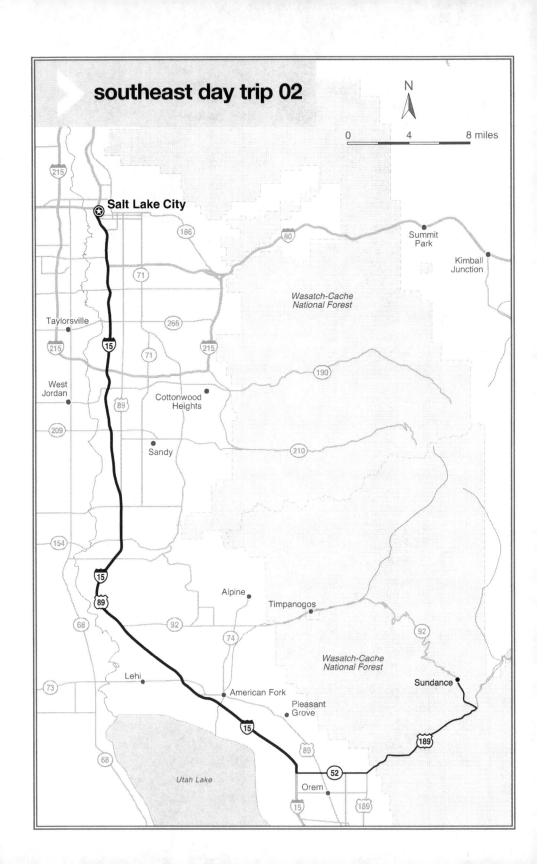

southeast day trip 02

N

0   4   8 miles

215

Salt Lake City

186

80

Summit
Park

Kimball
Junction

71

Wasatch-Cache
National Forest

Taylorsville

266

215

15

71

215

190

West
Jordan

89

Cottonwood
Heights

209

210

Sandy

154

15

Alpine

89

Timpanogos

92

68

92

74

Wasatch-Cache
National Forest

Lehi

73

Sundance

American Fork

Pleasant
Grove

189

15

89

68

52

Utah Lake

Orem

15

189

where to go

Sundance Resort. 8841 N. Alpine Loop Rd.; (866) 259-7468; www.sundanceresort.com. Nestled at the foot of Mount Timpanogos, Sundance Resort is a great destination for any and all seasons. Summers are packed with options for all ages and abilities. If you are an adrenaline junkie, mountain biking on the 25 miles of lift-serviced challenging terrain is available. The views from up here are breathtaking. While these trails are designed for the intermediate or advanced riders, there is also a Mountain Bike School available for riders of all abilities. If hiking is more your style, there are more than 10 miles of alpine hiking trails. Unlike the mountain biking, these are for everyone. It isn't cheating to take the lift to begin your hike—it is merely a way to expedite the excitement of enjoying the scenic trails. There will still be plenty of mountain left to climb as you peruse your way through the small upper valleys and waterfalls.

Do you want to truly unwind? The nearby Provo River has been rumored to contain up to 3,400 trout per square mile in certain sections. If you have never gone fly fishing, here is your chance to not only learn but be highly successful as well. Provo River Outfitters can provide a guided fly-fishing tour. A guide who knows the waters and can teach you the "dance" of fly fishing will make the day much more enjoyable. If you have the equipment and want to set out on your own, pick your spot and enjoy the day.

If two legs are good for hiking, then four are better, right? The stable is the place to either rediscover or maybe discover for the first time your cowboy side. This isn't your typical nose to tail ride; most trips take no more than 6 riders and will conduct you along some of the world's best trail systems. Get lost in your surroundings and scenery. Riders must be at least 8 years old. You also need to arrive 20 minutes early.

If one of these activities hasn't caught your attention, you might want to try river rafting, or maybe just relaxing on a scenic ride up the lift with a panoramic view. Or, maybe you want to unleash the creative side of you that's bursting to escape. Art classes are available daily at 10 a.m. and 1 and 3 p.m., by appointment only, by calling 24 hours in advance: (801) 225-4107, ext. 4335. These classes can be custom tailored to your interest and ability. Choose from a variety of arts including pottery, jewelry making, photography, watercolor or oil painting, and pencil drawing. See what creativity is lurking deep down inside that only a setting like Sundance can bring out of you. Additionally, enjoy a fascinating visit to the Glassblowing Studio, where you can watch molten balls of recycled glass transform into pieces of art. It's like watching poetry in motion.

Most famous for the home of the Sundance Film Festival, Sundance creates the perfect backdrop to the stars that shine above and below. Currently the majority of the festival is now held in Park City, but there are still a few events at the resort. This annual winter happening is a who's who of Hollywood and is a spectator's dream come true.

where to eat

Did we mention there was food? Dining at Sundance is also an art form. Taken from Mr. Redford's philosophy of organic, fresh produce, each meal is not only a work of art but also a culinary masterpiece.

Foundry Grill. Located at the resort's main building; (866) 932-2295. Open for breakfast, lunch, and dinner 6 days a week, and brunch and dinner on Sun. The Foundry Grill provides an upscale dining experience in a relaxed, more casual atmosphere. In the summer, weather permitting, enjoy patio dining. $$–$$$

Tree Room. Located at the resort's main building; (866) 627-8313. Open Tues through Thurs from 5 to 9 p.m. and Fri and Sat from 5 to 10 p.m. The Tree Room is elegance at its finest. This restaurant is the recipient of the prestigious AAA 4-diamond award as well as the *Wine Spectator* Award of Excellence. If you want a romantic, candlelit dinner, this is the place. And you never know who you might see here, especially during the Sundance Film Festival. $$$+

where to stay

Whether you lodge in a standard room or in a Mountain Suite, the rooms at **Sundance Resort** are incredible. They are fully equipped with wireless Internet, enabling you to post pictures of your vacation and brag to your friends on Facebook. Sundance also has a selection of Mountain Home rentals with 2 to 5 bedrooms. Indulge and stay a while—you won't want to leave. $$–$$$$

day trip 03

southeast

steamy engines:
heber city, midway

Heber Valley has everything you need for a fun outdoor day trip. Situated between the Wasatch and Uinta mountain ranges it is home to magnificent lakes, blue-ribbon trout streams, and some of the top-rated golf courses in the state. No matter what you do in the valley, you will soon realize how quiet and pleasant it is. Maybe it's the fresh air, maybe it's the high altitude, but life seems a little less hectic and a bit slowed down. The fun continues through the winter as well, with downhill skiing close at hand as well as the Olympic Cross Country Course in Midway. The valley is beautiful with plenty of snow. Pick an open field and see how big you can make your snowman.

Heber City is home to the Heber Creeper, whose route can take you to the base of Bridal Veil Falls and then back to Heber City—one of the most scenic ways to see Provo Canyon, without the traffic. Midway has that Swiss Alps feel and flair, even down to some charming Swiss chalets.

getting there

From Salt Lake City to Heber City is approximately 43 miles. Drive south on I-15 and take the I-80 east exit. Drive east on I-80 just past Park City. Take exit 146 (US 40) and travel south toward Heber City. As you enter Heber City on US 40, Midway is to your right.

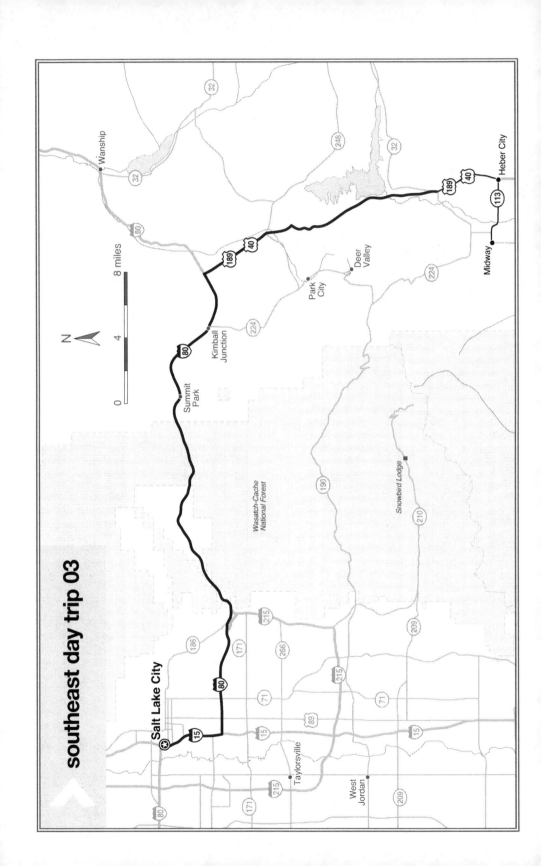

southeast day trip 03

where to go

Heber Creeper. 450 S. 600 West, Heber City; (435) 654-5601; www.hebervalleyrr.org. The historic Heber Creeper is one of the last steam-driven locomotive engines that still carries passengers. Feel like you stepped back in time as you board the train. Depending on your mood, the time of year, and your sense of adventure, this train has something for everyone.

Memorial Day weekend is a very special time when the kids can spend the day with Thomas the Tank Engine. This is an opportunity of a lifetime, to actually take a ride on Thomas himself. Besides Thomas, there are 15 other unique train rides available. If you're feeling a bit like Sherlock Holmes and you believe "a game is afoot," then the *Comedy Murder Mystery Dinner Train* is for you. The 2½-hour roundtrip train ride is filled with mystery, who done it, and lots of laughs. They also provide a delicious dinner while on board. If you're up for ghouls and trick-or-treats, the night ride during Oct will provide you with plenty of thrills. (Spooky, but still suitable for younger children.) Winter snows will bring on the thoughts of Christmas and a visit to Santa. The only way to get to Santa better than this is to ride his reindeer, but since this time of year they are in training for the big day, the next best thing is the *North Pole Express.* You need to reserve your tickets early because this ride sells out fast. Most of the train rides are between 35 minutes and 3 hours, and dates and times change from year to year depending on the excursion, so check their website for full details and how to book your adventure.

Keep in mind that there are combination excursions like the summertime *Raft 'n Rail,* combining a train ride, the river rafting of the cool Provo River, a visit to Sundance Resort, and a shuttle back to the depot. Also in the summer you can make a day of it with the *Reins 'n Trains* trips that combine a train ride with horseback riding. In the winter you can choose from 2 other fun and exciting trips. The *Tube 'n Train* combines snow tubing with tow-lift service and a scenic trip on the railroad through Soldier Hollow. Or, choose the *Sleigh Bells 'n Whistles* and experience the valley's winter wonderland as you travel both by rail and by sleigh. Advance reservations are required, 24 hours in advance, and discounted rates are available for groups of 20 passengers or more.

Reservoirs—Jordanelle, Deer Creek, and Strawberry. www.stateparks.utah.gov/parks. If you are looking for fun in the water, there are plenty of hosts to choose from and they are all close to Heber Valley. These reservoirs are stocked with fish, have great water-skiing or Jet Ski areas, plus great picnic areas. These are also excellent places for hiking and viewing the abundance of wildlife.

Soldier Hollow. Midway; (435) 654-2002; www.soldierhollow.com. With miles of groomed track, this is a great place for the beginning or expert cross-country skier. They have rentals and numerous instructors on hand for lessons if you're one of those who have only witnessed this sport from the comfort of your La-Z-Boy. If you need something a little more family friendly, enjoy the feeling of the wind in your face as you slide down one of the tubing lanes. If you find yourself at the bottom and don't have the energy to walk back up, don't worry; there are towrope lift services to tow you to the top of the hill. They say there are two seasons in Soldier Hollow: Snow Season and No Snow Season. If it is the latter, Soldier Hollow has you covered. In the summer there is mountain biking, hiking and horseback riding, or witnessing the Soldier Hollow Classic International Sheepdog Championship.

Midway. 75 N. 10 West, Midway. Midway was established as a stop halfway between Park City and Provo in the late 1800s. It's a quiet little town tucked into the mountain valley with hot springs to warm you and friendly people to welcome you. It was the choice settlement for many Swiss immigrants, and the architecture reflects this Swiss heritage. They have a Swiss Days celebration every year over Labor Day Weekend that brings artists, crafts, food, song, and dance to the main square. Make sure you plan a stop at the Homestead for their amazing handmade fudge, and catch a glimpse of the crater with its steaming hot springs. You can then burn all those calories at the 2002 Olympic venue, Soldier Hollow, whether by biking and hiking or cross-country skiing.

Midway is the home of the **Homestead Resort.** Adjacent to the resort is a 55-foot-tall beehive-shaped crater filled with geothermic hot springs. The Homestead Crater provides crystal-clear water formed 2 miles below the earth's surface. Enjoy swimming, scuba diving, or just soaking away the cold winter chill. They say the water comes from the same geothermic tubes that feed Yellowstone National Park, and the water remains a very warm 90 to 96 degrees year-round. Before scuba divers started exploring the crater, it was rumored the pool had no bottom. It is deep and most scuba divers descend 55 feet. The resort is also famous for its handmade fudge that comes in at least 16 different varieties. That alone is worth the drive! There is also golfing, fishing, wagon rides, or cross-country skiing.

where to shop

Heber City's Main Street has a wide assortment of boutiques and stores, selling everything from antiques and apparel to hardware and recreation equipment. You can be sure to find just about anything you might need.

where to eat

Blue Boar Inn. 1235 Warm Springs Rd., Midway; (888) 650-1400. A little off the beaten path, this eatery is reminiscent of a European pub. $$

Chick's Cafe. 154 S. Main St., Heber City; (435) 654-1771. Here, the diner-style food with a homemade touch is much better than fast food. But if you don't have time for a longer sit-down meal, they will get it out to you fast. Open daily. $

Dairy Keen (Home of the Train). 199 S. Main St., Heber City; (435) 654-5336; www.dairy keen.com. This might look like a typo, but this local hot spot is not related to Dairy Queen (although they do serve ice cream, burgers, and fries). The train going around the ceiling adds to its uniqueness. Trust us; it will keep the children and adults alike watching. $

Mountain House Grill. 79 E. Main, Midway; (435) 654-5370. This is where the locals eat when they aren't at home. It looks very Swiss on the outside but they have a little of every-thing on the menu. Try the Reuben sandwich, it is great! $

Taquiero Los Hermanos. 458 N. Main St., Heber City; (435) 654-2983. The building is as unique as the wonderful aroma of this Mexican restaurant. It is easy to find but open only for lunch and dinner. $$

where to stay

Holiday Inn Express. 1268 S. Main St., Heber City; (435) 654-9990; www.hiexpress.com/hotels/us/en/heber-city/hbcut/hoteldetail. This Holiday Inn is an excellent example of a hotel chain that has taken on the flair of the locals. This is a great place to stay. $–$$

Homestead Resort. 700 N. Homestead Dr., Midway; (866) 931-3097; www.homesteadresort.com. The Homestead will keep you busy during the day, so you might need to relax and stay the night. With rooms, deluxe suites, or individual cottages, they will make your stay exactly what you need it to be. $–$$$

Johnson Mill. 100 N. Johnson Mill Rd., Midway; (435) 654-4466 or (888) 272-0030; www.johnsonmill.com. Need a romantic getaway? The Johnson Mill is an amazing bed-and-breakfast. The mill was originally built in 1893 and was recently renovated to preserve its historic charm and style. The breakfast is sure to please! Stroll along the lake, enjoy the waterfall over the paddle wheel of the mill, or canoe out in the shade of Mt. Timpanogos. There are many weddings and events here, so book early! $$–$$$

Kastle Inn Bed and Breakfast. 1220 Interliken Lane, Midway; (435) 654-5987. Your hosts will do everything to make you comfortable, including provide a Pack 'n Play for a baby if you need it. The turret room has a jetted tub for a special evening, complete with sparkling cider! $$–$$$

Swiss Alpine Inn. 167 S. Main St., Heber City; (435) 654-0722; www.swissalpsinn.com. The charm of this little place invites you in, and the prices will keep you coming back. Con-veniently located in the middle of everything, this inn gets booked quickly—especially on the weekends, so make your reservations early. If you do catch them when they are full, the wonderful hosts will try to find a place for you. $

day trip 04

southeast

robbers roost:
wayne county,
capitol reef national park

One of the most scenic and beautiful places in the entire West, Wayne County is also one of the driest. It is the second driest county in Utah, and Utah is the second driest state in the US. This area is known as the "Land of the Sleeping Rainbow," with earthly colors changing from yellows to maroons to a reddish brown. Explore the outdoors at over 11,000 feet with incredible fishing lakes and plentiful wildlife.

One of the most famous stops in the county is Capitol Reef. In the 1920s these 378 square miles of colorful canyons, ridges, buttes, and monoliths were called "Wayne Wonderland." They also incorporated the 75 miles of rugged mountains from Thousand Lake Plateau southward to Lake Powell, which was called the Waterpocket Fold. Today this area is now preserved all within the 65-million-year-old Capitol Reef National Park. The true "Capitol Reef" is actually the magnificent and very rugged pieces of the Waterpocket Fold near the Fremont River.

getting there

From Salt Lake City, travel south on I-15 for 117 miles. Take exit 188 toward US 50/Scipio, then a left onto US 50. Follow US 50 by turning right on State Street in Scipio. Follow US 50 for 24.5 miles and turn right at SR 260, which is Main Street, leading into the town of Aurora. Follow Main Street until you reach SR 24 and turn right. Follow SR 24 for 2.8 miles and then take a slight left, staying on SR 24/State Street. Continue 44.4 miles and again take a slight left and continue on SR 24/300 south for 26 miles to the visitor center at Capitol Reef.

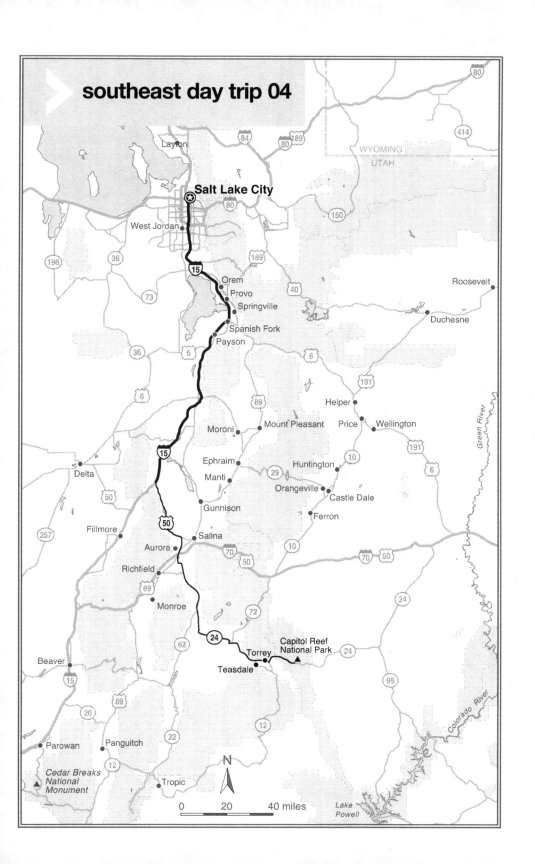

southeast day trip 04

what to do

Capitol Reef National Park. HC 70, Torrey; (435) 425-3791, ext. 111; www.nps.gov/care. In 1962 a road was constructed that finally provided easy access to this beautiful and colorful national park. Until this point, it was considered one of the most rugged and remote corners of the contiguous United States. You will appreciate how easy it is now to drive along SR 24 as it cuts through the park traveling east and west between Bryce Canyon National Park and Canyonlands National Park. The diversity of the park is endless, filled with shining white domes, cliffs, arches, canyons, layers of stone and earth, and sandstone cliffs that are brilliant in color. The Fremont River has cut canyons through much of the park, helping to create the diversity you see, but much of the beauty lies in the fact that it is still desert country.

For a scenic drive of the park's highlights, the paved path is short—really only a few miles. But if you don't mind unpaved and a little more adventurous roads and trails, there are hundreds of miles to explore.

You will find the park and campgrounds open year-round. With the exception of major holidays, the visitor center is open from 8 a.m. to 4:30 p.m., with extended hours during the summer from 8 a.m. to 6 p.m. There is an entrance fee for traveling the park's Scenic Drive. Individuals on foot or bicycles pay $3 per person, and vehicles and motorcycles pay $5; access is granted for 7 consecutive days. There may be a few extra fees for special use and backcountry permits; check with the Fee Office at (435) 425-3791, ext. 160, for details.

Capitol Reef offers a variety of pursuits, such as backcountry activities, biking, camping, horseback riding, and sightseeing. But the most popular activity is hiking and/or canyoneering. Hiking opportunities are available for all ages and abilities, and luckily some of the lower trails are wheelchair accessible. Because there are so many trails to choose from, here is a small sample of the more popular trails:

Easy:

- **Capitol Gorge.** As you walk in the narrow wash bottom, you will encounter sheer canyon walls, water pockets or "tanks," and Pioneer Register. (2.5 miles round-trip)

- **Goosenecks.** This hike will give you many panoramic views of Sulphur Creek Canyon. (0.5 mile round-trip)

- **Sunset Point.** You will want to plan this trip close to sunset as you will enjoy the dramatic lighting at the end of the day along with panoramic views of cliffs and domes. (0.7 mile round-trip)

- **Moderate:**

- **Cohab Canyon.** For the first 0.25 mile it may be a bit strenuous, but then it lightens up. You will climb to a hidden canyon with spur trails, overlooking Fruita. (3.5 miles round-trip)

- **Hickman Bridge.** This is a self-guided nature tour that leads you to the base of the incredible Hickman Natural Bridge. (2 miles round-trip)

Strenuous:

- **Cassidy Arch.** This hike will give you a bit of a steep climb from the Grand Wash to high cliffs, finally ending above the arch. (3.5 miles round-trip)

- **Frying Pan.** This hike gives you a 1,000-foot elevation change as you follow the ridge of Capitol Reef. (6 miles round-trip)

Other Activities in Old Wagon Trail

Following the old wagon route on Miners Mountain, you will see magnificent panoramic views of the Waterpocket Fold. (3.5 miles round-trip)

- **Mountain biking.** Staying on the designated roads at all times is a must in the park. Bicycles may not travel off road, in washes, on closed roads, on hiking trails, or backcountry routes. If you camp overnight, you must stay in 1 of the 3 selected park campgrounds. There are 4 detailed rides on the website. First is the **Scenic Drive,** which is easy to moderate with some hills and a length of 1 to 25 miles. The second is **Cathedral Valley Loop,** which is strenuous and 60-plus miles. The third ride is **South Draw Road,** which is strenuous with very steep hills and goes 12, 22, or 52 miles, depending on the route chosen. The fourth is **Boulder Mountain/UT 12-Burr Trail Road/Notom-Bullfrog Road/UT 24 Loop,** which is anywhere from 80 to 125 miles and very strenuous with steep hills.

- **Horseback riding.** If you wish to camp overnight with a horse, it must be within the Post Corral on an advanced-reservation basis only. They have a few recommended rides that you can find the details on when checking the website. You must have a backcountry-use permit, but it is free.

- **Camping.** Fruita Campground has 71 sites and is the only developed campground in the park. The fee is $10 a night, although seniors and Access Pass holders receive a 50 percent discount on their campsites. There are also the no-fee Cathedral and Cedar Mesa Primitive Campgrounds, which have no water and are in more remote parts of the park.

- **Rock climbing.** In the past, Capitol Reef National Park has seen minimal use by technical rock climbers. Over the past few years, however, there has been a surge in climbing in much of Utah.

- **Ripple Rock Nature Center.** The Nature Center has a variety of activities for hands-on learning for families and children. They are open Memorial Day weekend to June 30 from noon to 5 p.m. and July 1 to Labor Day weekend from 10 a.m. to 3 p.m., Tues through Sat (closed Sun and Mon).

robbers roost

"Robbers Roost" is also known as the Outlaw Trail. This was a route that incorporated rough, difficult stretches of landscape. Many of the best-known outlaws had a string of strongholds along this path that offered them an opportunity to rest after their "big job." Robbers Roost in the far northeastern area of Wayne County was one of these strongholds. Notables include Butch Cassidy, Kid Curry, and many other disreputable outlaws. Robbers Roost's unique topography allowed outlaws to move unnoticed and hide undetected when the law closed in. A spring still remains along with the remnants of the Cottrell cabin. Take yourself back in time as you explore the series of canyons in this area. To get to Robbers Roost, continue past Capitol Reef on SR 24 to Hanksville. Stay on SR 24 northeast about 15 miles. Robbers Roost will be on the right. www.canyoneeringusa.com /utah/roost

where to shop

The Historic Gifford Farmhouse. Located in Capitol Reef National Park. This wonderful farmhouse is part museum, part country store, with pioneer handicrafts. The best part is the amazing selection of homemade items sold daily: fruit pies, fresh-baked breads, old-fashioned soda pop, and ice cream. If you are craving a treat and need a break from the hot sun, they are open daily from 8 a.m. to 5 p.m.

Robber's Roost Bookstore. 185 W. Main St., Torrey; (435) 425-3265; http://robbers roostbooks.com. This bookstore was named after one of the favorite hideouts of Butch Cassidy and other outlaws. While reading from the diverse selection of books, you can hide out, too, and sit back and relax with some homemade baked goods and a drink. Open daily during the summer season.

where to eat

Cafe Diablo. 599 W. Main St., Torrey; (435) 425-3070; www.cafediablo.net. Cafe Diablo has earned an array of awards, including a Fodor's Choice Award and "Best Restaurant Southern Utah" from *Salt Lake* magazine, to name a few. The chef and owner graduated from the Culinary Institute of America in New York, and he has created some of the most succulent meals. They also have some of the most delectable homemade ice cream, breads, and pastries. If you are feeling adventurous, you will have to try the rattlesnake cakes—yes, they are truly made from real rattlesnakes! Open seasonally, Apr to Oct, daily from 5 to 10 p.m. $–$$

La Cueva Restaurante Mexicano. 875 N. SR 24, Torrey; (435) 425-2000; www.cafela cueva.com. At La Cueva the tortillas are made fresh daily, the salsas are handmade, and the entrees are truly delightful. The whole dining experience will satisfy. Open daily, with lunch from noon to 3 p.m. and dinner from 5 to 9 p.m. $

where to stay

The Lodge at Red River Ranch. 2900 W. SR 24, Teasdale; (435) 425-3322 or (800) 205-6343; www.redriverranch.com. This grand western lodge is distinctive in the way they blend the primitive past with modern-day convenience. With all the amenities of the present mixed with the heritage and rugged beauty of the Old West, you might think you stepped back in time. Because each suite has its own balcony and fireplace, you can really let go as you curl up by the fire or watch the sunset from your balcony. When staying at the Lodge, you will find that you are only minutes away from Capitol Reef National Park and Fishlake and Dixie National Forests, not to mention all the other wonders that southern Utah has to offer. $$$

Sky Ridge Inn Bed & Breakfast. 950 E. SR 24, Torrey; (435) 425-3222; www.skyridgeinn .com. This inn is nationally recognized for its service, artfully adorned and inviting rooms, and splendid views. After enjoying your full hot breakfast, you can explore to your heart's desire all the wondrous outdoor adventures that await you. $$

day trip 05

southeast

>>>

"grab the mountain bike, 4x4 & camera"
moab, canyonlands national park,
arches national park

moab

Do you consider yourself the adventurous type? Do you enjoy hiking, mountain biking, jeeping, climbing, or river rafting? If yes, Moab is definitely your day trip destination! A resort town, Moab is Utah's premier capital of adventure, offering something for everyone. Dance as if no one can see you at the Moab Music Festival, attend classical winery tours, or view numerous works of art at the local museums and galleries.

Don't forget about the Easter Jeep Safari, a weeklong affair, which is one of the largest events of the year. Jeepers embark on daylong trips hosted by the Red Rock 4-Wheelers, Inc. The club runs 9 different trails every day, with "Big Saturday" being the largest single trail ride. Departure on "Big Saturday" happens as 30 groups line themselves up and down town and head off in every direction for 30 different trails. Moab truly offers a variety of pastimes for all.

getting there

Moab is a bit of a drive from Salt Lake—four hours to be exact—but you will not be disappointed as you discover all the hidden "treasures" of southern Utah. From Salt Lake City, take I-15 South to exit 258 to merge onto US 6 East toward Price/Manit/US 89 East, and continue straight onto US 6 East/South State Road. Continue to follow US 6 East; then you will take the ramp onto 1-70 East and take exit 182 for US 191 South toward

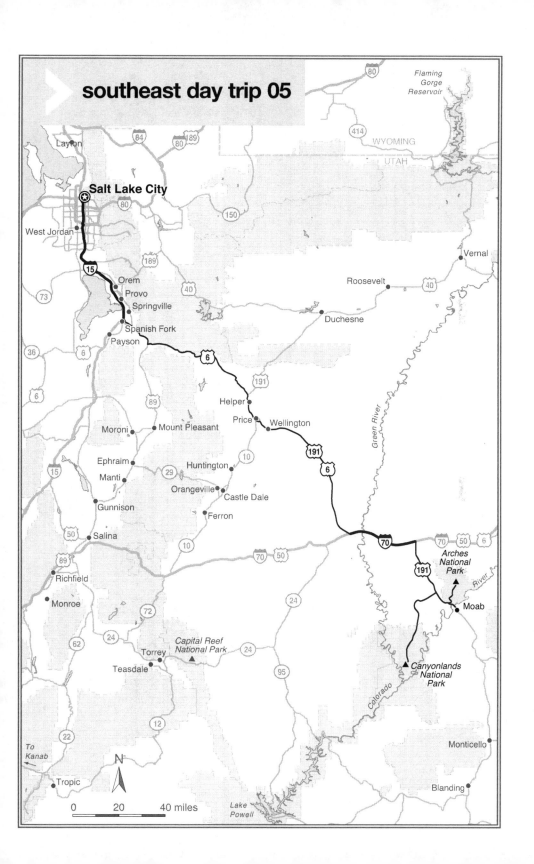

southeast day trip 05

Junction/Moab. Turn right at US 191 South, and then you will turn left at East Center Street in Moab.

where to go

Arches National Park. Located 5 miles north of Moab, Utah, along Highway 191; (435) 719-2299; www.nps.gov/arch. Arches is a must for all visitors to Moab! This park preserves over 2,000 natural sandstone arches and many other unusual rock formations. These rock layers display millions of years of geological events such as deposition and erosion. Two unusual natural features are common in Arches: biological soil crust and potholes. During the summer months family-oriented programs and activities are available each day. Check the visitor center for more details. Ranger-guided tours through the Fiery Furnace are offered twice daily from Mar to Oct, which is a popular 3-hour moderately strenuous hike. During this hike individuals will be walking and climbing on irregular and broken sandstone and along narrow ledges above drop-offs and in loose, sometimes wet sand. Make sure to go online to reserve your spot as hike slots fill several days in advance. Arches is open year-round, 24 hours a day. The visitor center is open daily from 7:30 a.m. to 6:30 p.m. Apr through Oct, 8 a.m. to 4:30 p.m. Nov through Mar, but closed Christmas Day. Individual passes are $5 (good for 7 days), vehicles are $10 (good for 7 days), or the Local Passport is $25 and good for 1 year admittance to Arches, Canyonlands, Hovenweep, and Natural Bridges.

Canyonlands National Park. Located at 2282 S.W. Resource Blvd.; (435) 719-2313; www.nps.gov/cany. Canyonlands displays a colorful landscape eroded into numerous canyons, mesas, and buttes by the Colorado River. The rivers divide the park into 4 districts: the Island in the Sky, the Needles, the Maze, and the rivers themselves. Each district offers

grand staircase-escalante national monument

Why this area was the last to be mapped in the continental United States is mind boggling as you view the majestic and magical landscape. The multi-hued cliffs and striking plateaus—all of which seem to run for such distances that they almost elude human perspective are breathtaking. There are 1.9 million acres that encompass the Grand Staircase-Escalante National Monument from its bewitching Grand Staircase of cliffs and terraces, across the Kaiparowits Plateau, to the magic of the Escalante River Canyons, and so much more. Get on your hiking shoes, grab your suntan lotion, camera, and have fun! 190 East Center, Kanab; (435) 644-4300.

different opportunities for exploration. There are no roads directly connecting the 4 districts. Although they may look close on a map, the districts require 2 to 6 hours of driving time due to the limited areas crossing the Colorado and Green Rivers. Some find it impractical to visit more than 1 or 2 districts in a single trip. Canyonlands is open 24 hours a day, year-round. Each district has its own visitor center. Island in the Sky's visitor center is open daily from 9 a.m. to 4:30 p.m., with extended hours Mar through Oct. The Maze's Hans Flat Ranger Station is open daily from 8 a.m. to 4:30 p.m. The Needles District Visitor Center is open daily from 9 a.m. to 4:30 p.m., with extended hours Mar through Oct. Closed Christmas and New Year's. Individual passes are $5 (good for 7 days), vehicles are $10 (good for 7 days), or the Local Passport is $25 and good for 1 year admittance to Arches, Canyonlands, Hovenweep, and Natural Bridges.

- **Hiking** can be done along the hundreds of miles of hiking trails. Here is where you can really explore the park's natural beauty. If you are looking for short hikes, day hikes, or backtracking trips, the **Needles** and **Island in the Sky** provide plenty of opportunities for any one of these.

- **Biking** in the Canyonlands means great mountain biking terrain, especially the 100-mile **White Rim Road** at the **Island in the Sky.** If you are not afraid of difficult roads and a multiday trip, then the **Maze** should be the adventure for you. Permits are required for all overnight trips in the backcountry but they are not required for day rides.

- **Horseback riding** is fine in **Horseshoe Canyon,** but cross-country travel is prohibited and you must have a permit.

- **Camping.** There are few options in the park. **Squaw Flat Campground** is ideal for a base camp for day hikers. The fee is $15 per night, and thankfully they do include bathrooms and water year-round. **Willow Flat Campground** is a short walk from one of the most spectacular sunset spots in the park, Green River Overlook. The fee is $10 per night with no water and only vault toilets.

- **Boating** down the Green and Colorado Rivers is one of the most interesting ways to see the park. These rivers played a major role in shaping the landscape of Canyonlands. Exploring the park by canoe, sea kayaks, and other shallow-water boats gives you miles and miles of flat water above the confluence. Below the confluence you will get the combined flow of both rivers as they spill down Cataract Canyon with amazing speed and power, with 14 miles of Class III to V white water. Permits are required for overnight private river trips. You can also check with the local outfitters, which offer a variety of guided tours, and choose from half-day excursions to weeklong floats. If you check on the Canyonlands website, you will have various outfitters to choose from.

- **4x4 and ATVing.** If you are looking for a little off-road adventure, you have many choices to choose from for 4-wheeling tour organizers and adventure travel packages.

Choose your once-in-a-lifetime off-road wheels: 4x4 Jeep, Hummer, or other 4WD vehicle, such as an ATV. If you check Google, you will find a plethora of choices for your off-road fun, but we have just included a few:

- **Moab Tour Company.** 543 N. Main St.; (435) 259-4080; http://moabtourcompany .us. If you want an informed and helpful staff to answer any of your questions, Moab Tour Company not only provides a spectacular selection of off-road rentals but will make sure you feel comfortable with what you choose. They offer many different tours, including the famous Moab Hummer Tour. Watch out National Parks, here you come!

- **Farabee 4x4 Rentals.** 401 N. Main St.; (435) 259-7494; www.farabeesjeeprentals .com. Farabee will help put together all you need for a jeep adventure of a lifetime. They have specially equipped jeeps that will allow you to explore the scenic backcountry roads or navigate the most rugged 4x4 trails.

- **Dead Horse Point State Park.** Located on SR 313 (18 miles off US 191 near Moab); (435) 259-2614; www.utah.com/stateparks/dead_horse.htm. The overlook at Dead Horse Point is 6,000 feet above sea level. Two thousand feet below, one can see the Colorado River winding itself a distance of 1,400 miles. From the overlook, canyon erosion may be seen as river slicing continues to sculpt the earth's crust. Water is limited at the park; it is suggested that visitors be prepared with water on hand. Fees: day-use pass $10, camping $20.

where to shop

Pinyon Tree Gift Shop. 82 S. Main St.; (435) 719-2086. This shop offers a variety of home decor and gifts. Their sandals are No. 1 in comfort and value. The Pinyon has a large selection of metal art, local pottery, and much more.

Rave'N Image. 59 S. Main St., Suite No. 5 (located in McStiff's Plaza); (435) 259-4968. The Rave'N Image is a family-run clothing business with style and selection. They carry clothing, bags, watches, belts, bath and body products, bathing suits, sunglasses, and the largest collection of jewelry in Moab. Open daily at 10 a.m.

StarShine Gifts. 37 E. Center St.; (435) 259-7778. StarShine offers stones and crystals, unique jewelry, books, music, and home decor.

The T-shirt Shop. 38 North Main St.; (435) 259-5271; www.moabtshirts.com. Designs and prints by local Moab artists. Make your own specialized T-shirt, bumper sticker, and more. This local shop adds creativity and charm to your souvenir experience.

where to eat

Bar-M Chuckwagon. 7000 N. US 191; (435) 259-2276; http://barmchuckwagon.com. Saddle up for some fun in the Old West. This restaurant offers a high-energy western dinner show full of humor and audience participation. Gunfights, games, and toe-tapping music are a part of your dining experience at the Bar-M. The chuckwagon menu includes sliced roast beef, barbecued chicken, baked potato, baked beans, cinnamon applesauce, buttermilk biscuits, old-fashioned cake, cowboy coffee or iced tea, and lemonade. Vegetarian menus are available. Open at 6:30 p.m.; the gunfight begins at 7 p.m., with supper at 7:30 p.m. sharp. The stage show follows supper. Normally open 2 to 4 nights per week in the spring season and 4 to 6 nights per week in the summer and fall. Season runs Apr to mid-Oct. Children 3 and under are free. $$

Milt's Stop & Eat. 356 Millcreek Dr.; (435) 259-7424. Enjoy an original classic diner, open since 1954. Open Tues through Sun 11 a.m. to 8 p.m.; closed Mon. Eat in or take out. Milt's Stop & Eat serves a variety of burgers, sandwiches, hot dogs, fries, chili, shakes, and malts. $

Moab Diner. 189 S. Main St.; (435) 259-4006; www.moabdiner.com. If you want a place where the locals eat, then Moab Diner is your place. With fast service and great food, this diner is a well-known secret in town. Open Mon through Sat, they offer a variety of delicious foods bound to satisfy even the pickiest of eaters. Enjoy such specials as Texas flatiron steak, breaded pork chops, *kokopelli* chicken dinner, or a "sweetwater skillet." Don't forget to try their famous green chili, voted best in Utah. $

The Sunset Grill. 900 N. Main St.; (435) 259-7146. Open Mon through Sat from 5 p.m. Sunset Grill, established in 1993, offers you a cliff-side dining experience. Using only fresh ingredients, this restaurant offers such dishes as Idaho trout, shrimp scampi, honey-pecan chicken, filet mignon, and more. $$

where to stay

Apache Motel. 166 S. 400 East; (800) 228-6882 or (435) 259-5728; apachemotel@frontier net.net. Take your picture with John Wayne, where he actually stayed for months at a time. Relax in modern deluxe rooms with great service and features. The Apache Motel offers free continental breakfast, free cable including HBO and ESPN in each room, a beautiful south-facing heated pool (seasonal), and free local calls. They're also pet friendly. $

Best Western Canyonlands Inn. 16 S. Main St.; (800) 649-5191 or (435) 259-2300; www .canyonlandsinn.com. Best Western Canyonlands Inn is a premier accommodation located in the heart of downtown Moab. Relax in the year-round heated pool and hot tub or work out in the fitness room. Best Western Canyonlands Inn offers free Wi-Fi, flat-screen televisions, and Euro Top mattresses in all of the rooms. They have a separate, secure mountain bike storage and maintenance room, a private children's playground, and a large spacious lobby. Make sure you call ahead as prices are dependent on dates of stay. $–$$

Cali Cochitta Bed and Breakfast. 110 S. 200 East; (435) 259-4961; www.moabdream inn.com. If you are looking for charming, quaint, and beautiful, the Cali Cochitta Bed and

Breakfast will fit that order. Plan on taking time to relax your sore feet by soaking in the hot tub after a day of hiking or ATVing, or just relax because you can. $$

Kokopelli Suites. 72 S. 100 East; (435) 259-7615 or (888) 530-3134; www.kokopellisuites .com. The Kokopelli offers 8 unique rooms with air-conditioning, refrigerator, microwave, cable television, secure bike storage, free Wi-Fi with guest computer, a community hot tub, and a barbecue area. Pet friendly ($5 per night per pet). $

Ramada Inn Moab. 182 Main St.; (435) 259-7141; www.ramadainnmoab.com. The Ramada Inn's southwestern-inspired guest rooms are especially designed to enhance subtle desert hues and earthy accents to provide you the perfect relaxation following a day of sightseeing and adventure. The inn offers an outdoor pool with spa, business services, and complimentary coffee and tea. Make sure to call ahead as room rates are dependent upon dates of stay. $–$$

River Canyon Lodge. 71 W. 200 North; (435) 259-8838; www.rivercanyonlodge.com. The River Canyon Lodge makes the most of your travel with amenities like free parking for boat trailers and ATVs, secure mountain bike parking, rooms with refrigerators and microwaves, and a cool sparkling outdoor pool. For families, they also offer roll-away beds, cribs, family suites and pet-friendly rooms. Complimentary coffee and tea in the lobby are available. Enjoy additional amenities such as a 12-person hot tub, high-speed Internet connection, and free local calls. Children under 12 stay free with an adult family member in the same room. Pet rooms are available with their pet policy. Call ahead for rates as room prices are dependent upon dates of stay. $–$$

south

day trip 01

south

happy valley:
provo

Although Provo is only 45 miles south of Salt Lake City, it has a very different feel. At its center is Brigham Young University and nearby Utah Valley University. With two universities, this bright, vibrant city is very much a college town. So it goes without saying, there is always something happening in Provo. If you are looking for museums, art exhibits, music performances, games, and cultural events all within walking distance of each other, this is your place.

Seven Peaks is always a local and day-tripper's favorite choice for cooling down when the summer heat becomes unbearable, or after you have hiked up the switchbacks to the "Y" on the mountain. Speaking of switchbacks, hiking is a local favorite pastime. You can push yourself by hiking up and around Pikes Peak or take it easy by walking toward Bridal Veil Falls in Provo Canyon.

Shopping is never a problem in Provo, as there are two large malls in the area and lots of smaller boutiques. Have you ever wondered how it felt to be a pioneer? Step back in time at Pioneer Village and let the Daughters of the Utah Pioneers help you find out. There is so much to see and do, and with the easy drive, you might want to plan multiple days exploring this part of the state.

getting there

From Salt Lake it is about 45 miles to Provo. Take US I-15 South to the Center Street exit 265. Travel east on Center to University and the heart of town.

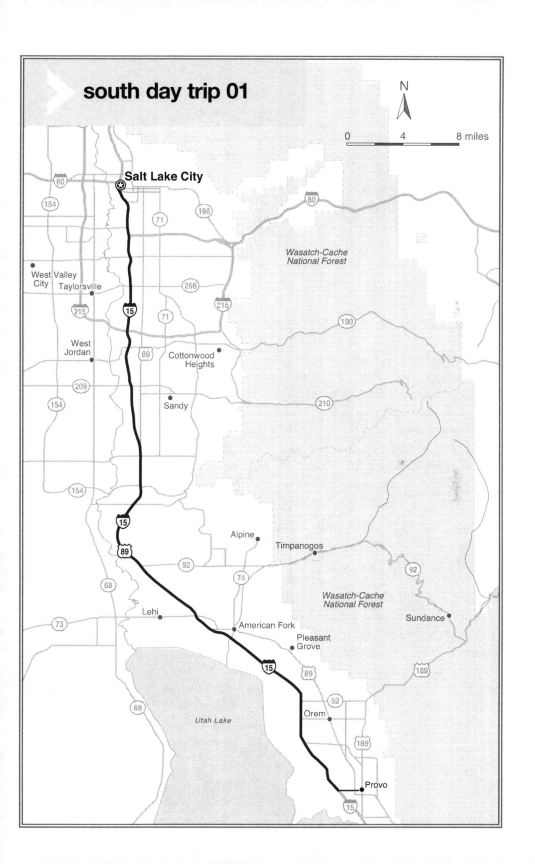

where to go

Daughters of the Utah Pioneers and Pioneer Village. 500 W. 600 North St.; (801) 852-6609. Take a step back to the era when settlers first came into the valley. Beautifully preserved and presented, the Daughters of the Utah Pioneers Museum provides a glimpse back in time. Not to be outdone, the Sons of Utah have created the Pioneer Village. Do you want to be thankful for the modern conveniences? Come see what it was like before cars, dishwashers, and, heaven forbid, cell phones and iPods. There are many things to see and do here at the museum and village, so bring the whole family. They are open beginning May 31, Mon 5 to 8 p.m., Tues through Fri 4 to 7 p.m., and Sat 1 to 4 p.m. There is no charge, but please feel free to provide a donation to help keep this heritage alive for future generations.

Monte L. Bean Museum. 645 E. 1430 North; (801) 422-5051; www.mlbean.byu.edu. You may have heard of a liger (lion/tiger mix), but have you ever seen one? The Bean Life Science Museum is home to Shasta the Liger and many other permanent exhibits and displays. From insects to waterfowl, you will see it all. In 1 day you will visit animals from Africa, China, Russia, and North America. Learn about the hunting methods of North American predators.

The museum tries to put you into the scene with natural and realistic panoramas of the way animals live. Get closer than you ever could in the wild. There is so much information that you can't visit without learning something new. You will enjoy the permanent exhibits, but check back for the schedule of upcoming and temporary exhibits. Hours: Mon through Fri 10 a.m. to 9 p.m. and Sat 10 a.m. to 5 p.m.; closed on Sun. Check their website as they often have special closing times.

Museum of Art at Brigham Young University. North Campus Drive; (801) 422-4322; http://moa.byu.edu. Walk in and you will see why this is one of the largest and best-attended art museums in the Mountain West. The art here is as art should be, ever changing and flowing from room to room. You never know what you are going to see next or even next week. The dynamic flow of the artwork itself keeps people coming time and time again. From the world-class traveling shows to the unique displays that will be shown on a temporary basis, you may be at a loss for words, but not memories. This is an art museum you won't have to worry about taking the kids to, either. The museum's commitment to excellence and integrity is evident in their displays, and there's nothing you need to worry about exposing anyone to. Modern art, classic art, sculpture, and expressionistic art are all here. With the uniqueness of the architecture of the building itself, you will find yourself immersed in art as never before. The museum is open Mon through Fri 10 a.m. to 6 p.m., Thurs evening 6 to 9 p.m., and Sat noon to 5 p.m. Closed on Sun.

Museum of Peoples and Cultures. 100 E. 700 North; (801) 422-0020; http://mpc.byu .edu. This quiet museum is open Mon through Fri 9 a.m. to 5 p.m. year-round. Walk the grounds of Brigham Young University and you will see the significance of this museum. The campus itself is buzzing with culture. Nearly every language and society either touches the campus or has influenced the students who attend BYU. The Museum of Peoples and Cultures is a direct expression of the world we live in. The exhibits change in Apr and are featured for 2 years. They are curated by the students and under the direction of the professional staff and BYU faculty. Students are so personally involved with the exhibits that when they take you on a tour they can get into very fine detail. Since general admission is free, you can return again and again if you don't have time to see it all. If you are interested in a docent-led tour, they are available for a minimal fee (cash or check only). Choose from Gallery Tours or Themed Tours with an accompanying hands-on activity. Cost ranges from $5 to $30 depending on the number of people in your group and the type of tour. Call the museum for more details.

Royden G. Derrick Planetarium. Room 465 on the fourth floor of the **Eyring Science Center,** BYU campus; (801) 422-5396; http://planetarium.byu.edu. Walk in while it is still broad daylight outside and surround yourself with the stars, planets, and galaxies inside, like you've never seen them before. The students from the astronomy department present weekly public planetarium shows every Fri at 7 p.m. and 8 p.m. in the planetarium. You will be so enthralled with the show you will want to stay for the night sky observation directly following. Shows change weekly so check the schedule and pick the one of most interest to you. The cost is only $2 and tickets are for sale at the door from 6:30 to 7 p.m. and again from 7:50 to 8 p.m. Cash or checks only.

eyring science center's star parties

If you are more in the mood for the real thing, you can enjoy the center's monthly star parties in the mountains east of Provo. There are other outreach and educational activities in the building as well, including a small dinosaur museum and some physics projects that kids can play with in various places. So much to see and do!

Bridal Veil Falls. US 189, East Provo Canyon Road, Provo Canyon. Breathtaking views of this 607-foot double cataract waterfall can be seen along the south side of the roadway. Parking is easy and free. At the base of the falls you will find a refreshing pool. Splash your cares away in the warm summer sun. The pool is shallow and the kids will love the excitement the waterfalls create. From here take one of the many hiking or biking trails. Don't forget your camera as the views are picture perfect. But what else would you expect from a bride on a sunny spring or summer day? The falls are ideal for a picnic and happen to be a riparian retreat for many birds, which will only add to the incredible experience and ambience. Additionally, they are a favorite spot in the winter for ice climbing. This isn't for the inexperienced; it is serious business, but fun to watch as climbers scale the frozen falls. If you have the experience and the equipment and the nerve, be ready for the thrill of a lifetime.

Seven Peaks Water Park. 1330 E. 300 North; (801) 373-8777; www.sevenpeaks.com. Situated in the heart of Provo and set against the backdrop of the towering mountains, this is the place where most of Utah comes to be "cool" in the summer (May to Sept). Hours are Mon through Sat 11 a.m. to 8 p.m. Half days also available 4 to 8 p.m. on select dates in Aug. This is Utah's largest water park, with 16 different waterslides to enjoy, a huge Wave Pool (500,000 gallons huge), kids' swimming areas and slides, group pavilions with cabanas, a giant Half Pipe tube ride, 100-foot Free Fall drop slides, and a ¼-mile Lazy River. We are out of breath just writing about it! Wait until you experience the thrill of being there. If you forgot your tubes, no problem—rentals are not only available but also very affordable. This is one of the few places where you can bring your lunch and picnic after you play.

where to shop

BYU Bookstore. Wilkinson Student Center (WSC), 1045 N. Campus Dr.; (801) 422-2400; www.byubookstore.com. Specialty candies, T-shirts or sweatshirts, and everything BYU, from logos to books. Everyone has a smile and is happy to serve you. The student center also has bowling, ice cream, an arcade, and other fun activities for the whole family.

Provo Towne Center. 1200 Towne Centre Blvd. (off I-15 and South University Avenue); (801) 852-2400; www.provotownecentre.com. So many shops, so little time! Enjoy a movie at the Megaplex Theater as well.

Shops at Riverwood. 4801 N University Ave.; (801) 802-8430; www.shopsatriverwoods .com. At the mouth of Provo Canyon, these shops are like a strip mall, but with beautiful walks all around. This is the place to get that hard-to-find gift for that hard-to-shop-for friend or relative. Wonderful restaurants also await you for that needed afternoon break in your shopping habit.

University Mall. 575 E. University Parkway (corner of University Parkway and State Street); (801) 224-0694; www.shopuniversitymall.com. Bring the kids and let them play in the life-size fabricated tree house in the center of the mall. Nordstrom, Macy's, and Dillard's all in one spot.

where to eat

Remember, this is a college town where food is king and all at prices college kids can afford.

Bombay House. 463 N. University Ave.; (801) 373-6677; www.bombayhouse.com. Want a day of culture? Why not stop by the Museum of Peoples and Cultures listed previously and then head to a delectable cultural delight at the Bombay House on University Avenue. The smell is intoxicating, the food is wonderful, and the waiters are authentic. The atmosphere will have you transported, and when you try the *naan* bread or chicken *tikka masala* you will believe you really have been to India. $$

Brick Oven. 111 E. 800 North; (801) 374-8800; www.brickovenprovo.net. Pizza and pasta are the perfect combination, but when you bake the pizza in a brick oven like mama did back in Italy, it is extraordinary! They will usually seat you pretty quickly, but if you have a group larger than 8 you might want to call ahead for reservations. Keep in mind, however, that they don't make reservations on Fri and Sat evenings after 3:30 p.m. They have party seating for group sizes up to 18, 34, or 60 in their private rooms. $

BYU Creamery 9th Street Grill. 1209 N. 900 East; (801) 422-CONE. It may look like a grocery store, but this is a great place to stop for a grilled sandwich and the best ice cream in Provo. $

J Dawgs. 858 N. 700 East; (801) 373-3294. If you love Chicago-style hot dogs, then this stop is a must while you are near BYU. The "dawgs" have a unique diamond pattern that creates a crisp outside—it is unmatched in the valley. Add your choice of toppings, just how you want it, and your mouth will be watering before the first bite goes in. $

Los Hermanos. 16 W. Center St.; (801) 375-5732. This is probably the best Mexican food in town. It is located in the heart of downtown and close to everything. Start off with their fresh tortilla chips and salsa—you won't be able to stop eating them. When you order, you need to try the Diablo Verde and see if you can figure out the secret fifth ingredient. From chili *rellenos* to chicken *taquitos,* you will not leave here hungry. $

where to stay

Hines Mansion Bed & Breakfast. 383 W. 100 South; (801) 374-8400, (800) 428-5636; www.hinesmansion.com. This is not your average bed-and-breakfast. "Charm" and "authentic elegance" are the best words to describe this inn tucked away in the city center. Here, you will enjoy the luxurious warmth of the Hines Mansion and be pampered by the friendly staff and owners. Check out the website and see the different rooms to choose from. If you are going to stay in Provo, make it extra special. $$–$$$$

Marriott Hotel. 101 W. 100 North; (800) 777-7144; www.marriott.com/provo. This hotel is perfect if you want to be in the middle of everything. The prices are reasonable for a full-service Marriott, and the staff is friendly. $

day trip 02

south

where inspiration was born:
bryce canyon national park

There are many mysteries about Bryce Canyon, such as the way the columns seem to rebel against Mother Nature herself. To the locals they are called "hoodoos." To the visitor they look like something right out of Dr. Seuss. Either way they are the reason people come back to Bryce Canyon time and time again. Looking out over this arid basin you will see these tall skinny spires of weathered rock that protrude from the bottom of this beautiful red canyon. These are the hoodoos. They appear many places throughout the world but nowhere is there such an abundance of them as the northern section of Bryce Canyon National Park. The best place to see the hoodoos is to view them as you hike the trails that descend into the canyon.

There are practically no words to describe Bryce Canyon, as it is really nature's wonderland. *Canyon* is misleading since Bryce was not carved by a river but rather through "frost-wedging" and chemical weathering (better known as the freeze thaw). It's one of the most photographed places in Utah, and the contrast in colors, especially when set against a clear blue sky, is something more than spectacular. Add to it a light dusting of snow and you really have a pretty picture.

getting there

From Salt Lake City, head south on I-15 for 213 miles. Take exit 95 and turn left on UT 20, traveling east. Go 20.5 miles and turn right on US 89, traveling south. In the town of Panguitch, turn left on Center Street, (US 89) and go 6.9 miles. Turn left on UT 12, drive 13.5 miles and turn right on UT 63, traveling south. Drive 3 miles to Bryce Canyon National Park.

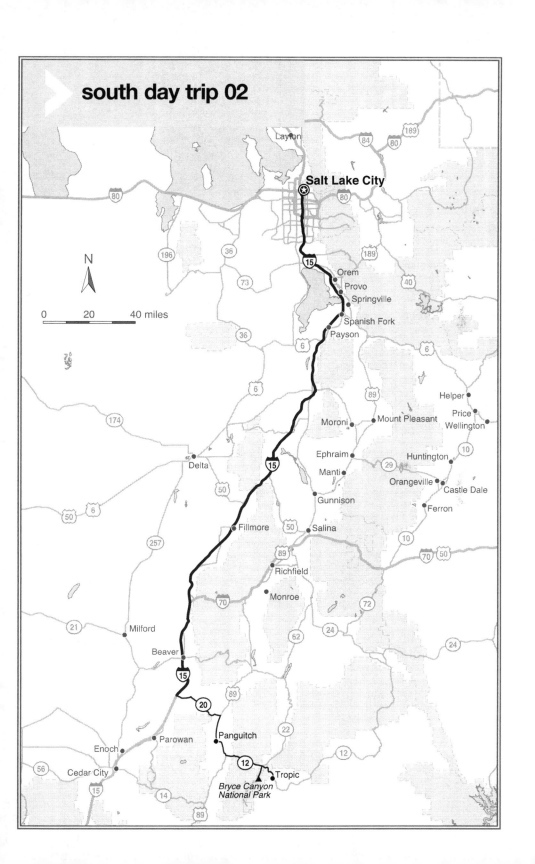

south day trip 02

what to do

Bryce Canyon National Park. SR 63, Bryce; (435) 834-5322; www.nps.gov/brca. Operating hours depend on all 4 seasons: summer (May through Sept) 8 a.m. to 8 p.m., fall (Oct) 8 a.m. to 6 p.m., winter (Nov through Mar) 8 a.m. to 4:30 p.m., spring (Apr) 8 a.m. to 6 p.m. They are closed on Thanksgiving, Christmas, and New Year's Day. The entrance fee to Bryce Canyon National Park is $25 for each private vehicle. If you are entering by foot, bicycle, or motorcycle, they require that you pay $12 per person. But don't forget, just as at the other national parks, the admission is good for 7 consecutive days. Because things can be very congested, you have the option of riding their free shuttle service. Bryce offers a variety of activities, such as backcountry adventures, biking, camping, snowshoe hikes, astronomy programs, kids programs, horseback riding, sightseeing, and more. Much like the other national parks, some of the most popular activities are canyoneering and hiking. There are hiking opportunities available to all ages and abilities, and luckily some of the lower trails are wheelchair accessible. Here are just a few of the more popular trails:

Easy:

- **Mossy Cave.** Walk alongside a stream to a small waterfall and mossy overhang. (0.8 miles round-trip)

- **Rim Trail.** This path allows you an alluring view of hoodoos from above as you walk a fairly tame trail. (11 miles round-trip)

- **Bristlecone Loop.** Hike through forests of spruce fir to bristlecone pine precipices and beautiful vistas. (1 mile round-trip)

Moderate:

- **Navajo Trail.** This trail is open on both sides, beginning at Sunrise Point and descending down in the canyon past Thor's Hammer and Two Bridges. To finish up your hike you will come through a slot canyon, Wall Street, and a winding trail to the top. (1.3 miles round-trip)

- **Tower Bridge.** Along this trail you will see the bristlecone pines and the China Wall. (3 miles round-trip)

- **Hat Shop.** Hike down until you are on the Under-the-Rim Trail, where you will see a cluster of balanced-rock hoodoos. (4 miles round-trip)

Strenuous:

- **Fairyland Loop.** Believe it or not, the Fairyland Loop is a less-crowded trail that shows you the China Wall, Tower Bridge, and more tall hoodoos. (8 miles round-trip)

- **Peek-A-Boo Loop.** This stunning but steep trail takes you through the heart of Bryce Amphitheater, and you will see the Wall of Windows. (5.5 miles round-trip)

- **Riggs Spring Loop.** Once you leave Rainbow Point, you will hike through varied forests of bristlecone, spruce, and fir. Come prepared as this is a high-elevation hike. (8.5 miles round-trip)

Other Activities in Bryce Canyon:

- **Horseback riding.** (435) 679-8665. You can take a different type of "hike" from atop a horse. Wranglers from Canyon Trail Rides will lead you in a 2- or 4-hour horse or mule ride into Bryce Amphitheater and along the Peek-A-Boo Loop Trail.

- **Camping.** Close to the visitor center you will find Bryce's only 2 campgrounds, North and Sunset. Not only do they have some of the world's true wonders—flushing toilets—they also have drinking water. Where do we sign up? If you are fit to be showered, during the summer months there is a coin-operated laundry and shower facilities at the General Store nearby. All sites are limited to 10 people at a cost of $15 a night, and holders of special park passes receive a 50 percent discount. If you are adventurous enough to want some backcountry camping, there are limited sites available.

- **Snowshoe hikes.** During the winter you can opt for a guided snowshoe hike, and they even supply the snowshoes.

anasazi state park museum

Are you looking for a rather rustic summer home? There are plenty to choose from at the Anasazi State Park. Then again, maybe just a summer visit is a better choice. This is home to one of the largest Ancestral Puebloan communities west of the Colorado River, and it sits right in the center of Utah's canyon country. This ancient village is believed to have housed more than 200 people from AD 1160 to 1235. More than 100 structures and thousands of artifacts have been uncovered, and some are even displayed in the museum. Open Apr through Oct from 8 a.m. to 6 p.m. and Nov through Mar from 9 a.m. to 5 p.m. Closed Thanksgiving, Christmas, and New Year's Day. Fee: $5 per person or $10 per family. 460 N. UT 12, Boulder; (435) 335-7308; www.stateparks.utah.gov/parks/anasazi.

where to shop

Old Bryce Town Shops. 26 S. Main St., Bryce Canyon City; (435) 834-5341 or (866) 866-6616; www.rubysinn.com. The remarkable stores at the Old Bryce Town Shops will give you that Wild West feel. If you have never seen an authentic western town, you will truly enjoy meandering through the shops and finding unique gifts for family and friends. Relish some homemade cookies, candies, or ice cream or check out their selection of holiday items and home decor. The General Store holds almost anything a real cowboy or cowgirl would need or want, and don't forget the Canyon Rock Shop, where you can find that one-of-a-kind gift. Open year-round.

Red Canyon Indian Store. Panguitch; (435) 676-2690; www.redcanyon.net. Little Red Chief may be out for the day, but you are sure to find some of the most extraordinary souvenirs, Native American gifts, or Indian artifacts. Not only will you find some fun treasures to take home, but you can take a break by enjoying some refreshments and sandwiches at the deli.

where to eat

Bryce Canyon Inn Restaurant. 21 N. Main St., Tropic; (435) 679-8888; www.brycecanyon inn.com. Grandma, we're home! The Bryce Canyon Inn Restaurant will remind you of eating at Grandma's house, with down-home cooking at its best. You can choose to dine on the patio while you enjoy the cool mountain evenings or bask in the morning sunshine. Open from Mar through the end of Oct for breakfast, lunch, and dinner. $

Ebenezer's Barn and Grill. 26 S. Main St., Bryce Canyon City; (435) 834-5341 or (866) 866-6616; www.rubysinn.com/ebenezers. Put on your cowboy boots and get ready for a boot-kickin', toe-tappin' good time as you join in the western music and fun at Ebenezer's. You will really feel like you have gone back to the Old West. If you aren't too tired after your delicious dinner, you can get up and move those feet to the music. Includes dinner and entertainment. Open year-round. $$

Hell's Backbone Grill. 20 N. UT 12, Boulder; (435) 335-7464; www.hellsbackbonegrill .com. Here you will find the perfect blend of western range, Pueblo Indian, and southwestern cuisine and flavors. When you come to Hell's Backbone Grill, you will experience these amazing tastes and smells as food is transformed into art. You'll taste the freshness in every bite because they grow much of their own organic produce and herbs. Their meats are also locally raised and natural. When it comes to their desserts, be prepared to swoon over choices that cause a flavor collision between heaven and Earth—regardless of the restaurant's name. Open mid-Mar through Thanksgiving. $$

where to stay

Bryce Canyon Inn. 21 N. Main St., Tropic; (435) 679-8502 or (800) 592-1468; www.bryce canyoninn.com. You will really enjoy the time you spend at the Bryce Canyon Inn, especially after a long day of visiting the vast display of colorful rock formations. Their new private log cabins are tastefully decorated for the "cowpoke" in everyone, each with its own private bath, cable TV, refrigerator, and more. The staff will make you feel at home and you will want to come again. All of this ambience doesn't come at a high price, either; these delight-ful cabins are very affordable. All rooms and cabins include a complimentary continental breakfast. Open from Mar through the end of Oct. $

Stone Canyon Inn. 1220 W. 50 South, Tropic; (435) 679-8611 or (866) 489-4680; www .stonecanyoninn.com. Stone Canyon Inn is where Paradise meets Paradise. You will be in awe and wonder as you experience their unsurpassed accommodations (they also offer cabins). Sit back and relax in the Jacuzzi at the end of a long day of hiking, or simply enjoy the incredible view from your private room. Waking up is a pleasure when you know that you will have a 5-star breakfast waiting for you. Open year-round except for Jan. $$

day trip 03

south

"much ado"
cedar city

Cedar City was first named Fort Cedar when it was just a small settlement because of the abundance of trees that were called "cedar" trees. The interesting part of this story is that those trees were simply junipers.

There is "much ado" in Cedar City—possibly so much that William Shakespeare himself could have lived here. To the residents and thousands of visitors each year, some think he does—in spirit at least. He is the cornerstone of the Utah Shakespeare Festival, which has been an annual mainstay in Cedar City for 50 years.

Along with catching a performance or two inspired by the Bard, you might also want to join excitement of the Utah Summer Games. This annual Olympic-style sports festival involving some 50 different sports is sponsored by Southern Utah University and attracts athletes from across the state.

Because of the numerous festivals that take place in Cedar City, it has become known as "Festival City USA." The list includes the American Children's Christmas Festival, Groovefest, SkyFest, the Neil Simon Festival, the Great American Stampede, the Cedar City Livestock and Heritage Festival, July Jamboree, the Utah Midsummer Renaissance Faire, and the Paiute Restoration Gathering, to name a few. There is obviously always something new to do.

Cedar City is a great place to stage your "base camp" as you explore the many magnificent southern Utah natural wonders. Cedar Breaks National Monument, Brian Head Ski Resort, Parowan Gap Petroglyphs, and scenic byways are only the beginning.

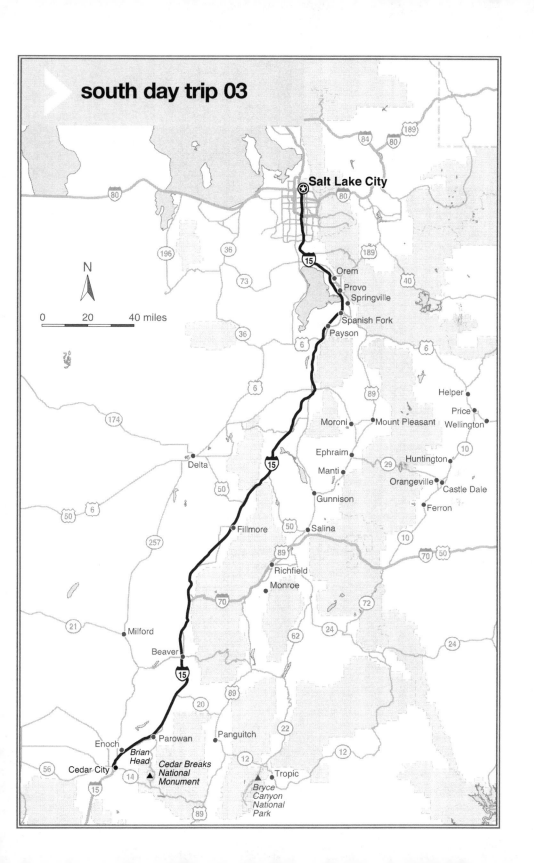

south day trip 03

N

0   20   40 miles

Salt Lake City

15

Orem
Provo
Springville
Spanish Fork
Payson

189

40

84
189

80

80

196

36

73

36

6

6

174

Delta

50

50   6

257

Fillmore

Moroni   Mount Pleasant
Ephraim
Manti

89

29

Gunnison

50   Salina

89

Richfield

Monroe

70

Helper
Price
Wellington

10

Huntington
Orangeville   Castle Dale
Ferron

10

70   50

72

21

Milford

Beaver

15

24

62

24

20

89

22

Enoch
Cedar City

56

15

14

Parowan

Brian
Head   Cedar Breaks
National
Monument

Panguitch

12

12

Tropic

Bryce
Canyon
National
Park

89

15

getting there

Travel south from Salt Lake City on I-15 for 248 miles. Take exit 56 east to the heart of the city. Turn right on Main Street.

where to go

Shakespeare Festival. 351 W. Center St.; (435) 586-7880; www.bard.org. The Utah Shakespeare Festival is held each summer and fall amid the beauty only Shakespeare and southern Utah can create. Enjoy a variety of performances in the Adams Memorial Shakespearean Theatre, one of the most authentic Elizabethan theaters in the world. As you sit to watch a performance, you'll feel you've been transported to the Globe in London, sitting at the very theater where William Shakespeare unfolded his masterpieces so many years ago. In fact, the Adams Memorial Shakespearean Theatre so closely resembles Shakespeare's Globe Theatre that a British Broadcasting Company chose to film some of its Shakespeare series in Cedar City. You will have to ask yourself whether or not you are meant to visit Cedar City; is it "to be or not to be: that is the question"?

As they say in Cedar City, "What is life without a little play?" Winning the Tony Award for "Outstanding Regional Theater" in 2000 was a highlight for the Utah Shakespeare Festival. This is widely known as one of the best professional theater events in the nation. Not only are the plays expertly produced by talented professionals, but they also employ some of the most talented and seasoned actors and actresses from all over the United States.

While attending the festival, take time to enjoy the free actor, literary, and prop seminars, backstage tours, and play orientation before each show. During the backstage tours you will learn about the central workings of the festival and visit the many different production areas, such as the costume, makeup, and scenery shops.

If you are a theater buff and have ever had a question you were dying to know the answer to but never had a chance to ask, you can finally get your opportunity when you attend a Curtain Call Lunch. Here you will have the occasion to listen to an actor, designer, director, or other festival luminary. The lunches are at noon each Fri in July and Aug. The tickets can be purchased just prior to lunch.

Each evening before the productions, visitors are invited to attend the **Green Show,** which is held at the courtyard surrounding Adams Theatre, for free. You will feel the mood and merriment in the midst of music, dancing, and entertainment, all to your heart's content. Sit back, enjoy a treat, and relax before the show begins.

The Utah Shakespeare Festival runs from the end of June through the end of Oct; call or visit their website for more details on pricing and performance information.

Cedar Breaks National Monument. 2390 W. UT 56, Suite 11; (435) 586-9451; www.nps .gov/cebr. Don't have time to fully appreciate Bryce Canyon? The next best thing is a visit to Cedar Breaks National Monument, the "Mini-Me" of Bryce Canyon National Park. It is said by some visitors to have even more brilliant colors than Bryce Canyon, and the "Circle of Painted Cliffs" is what the Indians called Cedar Breaks because of the vibrant rich colors along so many of its cliffs. Cedar Breaks is much like a huge amphitheater with a 2,000-foot drop to the floor, where the stone spires, columns, arches, and pinnacles give the unique detail of the canyons. Not only will you enjoy the intricate and varying shades of color found in the canyon—the reds, purples, and yellows—but you also will be in awe by the stunning wildflower display that early summer brings.

There are many recreational activities that can be relished as you sightsee, hike, study nature, picnic, camp, or just take photos. Most trails are considered easy but they may be strenuous for the elderly, persons not in good physical condition, or those with respiratory problems. This is a distinctive place for cross-country skiing and snowmobiling during the winter with access to Brian Head Resort.

Cedar Breaks National Monument is 23 miles east of Cedar City and only 3 miles south of Brian Head Resort. During the winter, if you need a break from cross-country skiing, snowshoeing, or snowmobiling, you can warm yourself by the fire at the Winter Warming Yurt that serves as a winter ranger station. Open from late May to mid-Oct. Entrance fees are $4 per adult; children under 16 are free.

Brian Head Resort. 329 S. UT 143, Brian Head; (435) 677-2035; www.brianhead.com. The Travel Forum rated Brian Head as a "Top Family Getaway for Family Travelers." Brian Head touts being Utah's highest elevation resort, receiving more than 400 inches (over 33 feet) of light powder every year. They have over 50 runs for all abilities, runs that include the entire mountain and are great for beginners and children. For those who want a little extra winter thrill, they have 4 terrain parks with different ability levels—rails, fun boxes, and a half pipe are just a few of the 30 snow features offered there.

If skiing isn't your cup of tea, what about sliding down a mountain on a tube? On this mountain you don't have to worry about the hike up, either. Brian Head has a lift-served Snow Tubing Park featuring 6 lanes to choose from. Talk about a winter wonderland! Slide to your heart's content. Brian Head Resort offers so many exciting options, choosing will be the hard part. In addition to snowboarding and skiing, they have sleigh rides, spa treatments, snow tubing (with the lift), snowmobiling, ski school, snowshoeing, and more. They also offer a plethora of lodging options that should please every budget. You may find that Brian Head Resort is one of the best kept secrets in Utah! Open for the ski season from Nov to the end of Apr, 9:30 a.m. to 4:30 p.m.

Frontier Homestead State Park Museum. 585 N. Main St.; (435) 586-9290; www.utah .com/stateparks/iron_mission.htm. Frontier Homestead State Park Museum, or Iron Mission State Park as it used to be named, mostly tells of the unique and difficult development of Iron County. Mining for iron is how it all began, and here you will get a feel for the early settlers of this region. The museum features horse-drawn vehicles used in the 1850s to the 1920s and has a wonderful collection of pioneer and Indian artifacts. There is a picnic area available along with hiking and biking trails close by. A $3 day use fee is required for entrance.

Parowan Gap Petroglyphs. 176 E. D. L. Sargent Dr.; (435) 586-2401; www.scenicsouthern utah.com/heritage_discovery/parowangap.shtml. Here you will see artwork chipped into the smooth side of large boulders. These petroglyphs date back several centuries and are the work of the Native Americans who once inhabited this region. Each of them tells a story, and if you can read them you will win many accolades, as the argument on what they really mean has been long debated by many archaeologists. Walk as lightly as you can while witnessing these wonders, for the Parowan Gap Petroglyphs are considered cultural treasures; if any are damaged, their meaning would be lost to us forever.

Snowmobiling. Do you want to catch a little air, feel the wind in your face, or view some beautiful country? Snowmobiling will provide you with a thrill of a lifetime. The Cedar Mountain/Duck Creek Village east of Cedar is a wonderland for snowmobilers. Cedar Mountain and the desert areas west of town also offer exceptional ATV trails.

Hiking. www.utah.com/cedarcity/hike.htm. With so many superb places to enjoy the scenic hikes through valleys and hills and over mountains, you should check out the website above to find the one that best suits you.

where to shop

Bulloch Drug. 91 N. Main St.; (435) 586-9651; www.bullochdrug.com You might be surprised to find this is no ordinary drug store. Bulloch is an experience, and one the whole family will find entertaining! Bulloch Drug is located in heart of Cedar City. If you don't need to visit the pharmacy, no worries—there is much more to keep your attention.

In the late 1950s and early 1960s the store not only housed a long soda fountain but also a cafe. The cafe became a real gathering hot spot for the locals, along with the upstairs, which was used for social events like dinners, dances, and luncheons.

Today the center of the store houses the Soda Fountain, which is an original 1942 model that has been restored. If you have never tried a true Ironport soda, be sure to order one; this is a soft drink served mostly in the West that tastes like cream soda with a kick—a real western kick! Within Bulloch's you will also find Comforts of Home, offering a variety of home decor, gifts, and collectibles. And if all that is not enough to fit into 1 store, they also have the Wood 'N Lace Place, which is a great little boutique carrying handbags, jewelry, beads, scarves, the Marie Osmond Collection, and numerous other accessories.

Groovacious. 173 N. 100 West; (435) 867-9800; www.groovacious.com. This fun and "rocking" music store will keep your foot tapping and your fingers snapping to the beat. You could happily spend the entire afternoon looking around for that perfect music mix, song, or musical item. Open daily except Sun.

Utah Shakespeare Festival Gift Shop. 351 W. Center St.; (435) 586-7878. If you look, you will undoubtedly find something from the gift shop for extra lasting memories. You can also find a diverse selection of one-of-a-kind gifts, knickknacks, jewelry, bags, children's gifts, books, souvenirs, clothing, and more. This shop is filled with fun and whimsical items, with something for everyone! Open only during the Utah Shakespeare Festival.

The Wizz. 490 S. Main St.; (435) 586-7113. You could consider this shop an eclectic alternative gift store. You can find everything from fairies and dragons to wind-chimes and frames to incense and romantic jewelry. If you have any kids in tow, you may want to steer clear of the back of the store as you never know what you might find!

where to eat

The Garden House. 164 S. 100 West; (435) 586-6110. This quaint little cottage touts good home cooking with a hint of elegance. Take pleasure in the great atmosphere of this restaurant off the beaten path. Relax for dinner in their outdoor seating area, or enjoy this gem from inside the main dining area. While there, don't forget to order one of their special-ties, fruited lemonade, in flavors such as blueberry or strawberry. Open every day from 4 to 9 p.m. $–$$

Maggie Moo's Ice Cream and Treatery. 1760 N. Main St., No. 101; (435) 865-6839; www.maggiemoos.com. Watch out for Maggie, who is always decked out in her pink dress and pearls, though you might be surprised to find she is a cow. If you have ever seen the ice-cream cupcake featured on the Food Network, or tried their ice-cream pizza, you will know that they are not only known for innovation but for fun as well. No matter what your ice-cream indulgence might be, you will find it at Maggie's: 3 "udderly" fabulous flavors of Maggie Mia's ice-cream pizzas (Supreme, Chocolate Lover's, Cheese—alias white-chocolate curls), ice-cream cupcakes, smoothies, milk shakes, cakes, and more. Using their award-winning ice cream, they fold in your favorite nuts, candy, or fruit by hand to make the perfect treat. $

Milt's Stage Stop. 3560 E. UT 14; (435) 586-9344; http://miltsstagestop.com. This rustic log cabin is tucked away into the beautiful mountains of Cedar City, only 10 minutes from town yet seemingly in a whole different world. Enjoy steak and seafood at this calming, refining, and relaxing restaurant in the back mountains. Come and relish the ambience of the West! Open daily from 5 to 9 p.m. $$

Pastry Pub. 255 N.W. Center St.; (435) 867-1400; www.cedarcitypastrypub.com. Owners Syrus and Kim Saifizadaeh created their business around a French pub theme. For over 10 years now, this local favorite has been dishing up their specialties, beginning with pastries but now with a variety of other items (not that some people can't survive on pastries alone). They have a delicious array of choices, from sandwiches, wraps, and croissants to soups and vegetarian dishes. Stop by one day when you have a little time to unwind and enjoy some of the best pastries you have ever encountered while you check your e-mail (Wi-Fi is free). Open daily, except Sun, from 10 a.m. to 10 p.m. $

Rusty's Ranch House. 2275 E. UT 14; (435) 586-3839; www.rustysranchhouse.com. If you're thinking meat, look no further than Rusty's Ranch House for satisfaction. They'll have you shouting, "Yahoo!" They serve everything from seafood to steaks, with many things in between, even offering "Tumble Weed." To find out what that means, you'll have to pay them a visit. Open Mon through Sat from 5 p.m.; closed on Sun. $–$$

where to stay

Amid Summer's Inn. 140 S. 100 West; (435) 586-2600; www.amidsummersinn.com. This lovely historic English Tudor bed-and-breakfast will truly take you back in time, with a quaint tree-lined street and romantic look and feel. You can enjoy dinner at the gourmet restaurant just 2 doors down or walk just a block away to the Tony Award–winning Utah Shakespeare Festival. Gary and Charlene, your hosts, are dedicated to making sure your stay is full of memories and leisure as they tend to your every need. Amid Summer's Inn has earned international acclaim, being voted the "Inn of the Year" in 2009 (by *The Complete Guide to Bed and Breakfast, Inns and Guesthouses International*). Every room features a queen or king bed with a private bath, and some suites come with a large jetted tub. You will be able savor every bite of the multicourse, warm gourmet breakfast, either family-style or on the covered deck. Amid Summer's Inn could have you dreaming even before you arrive. $$

Iron Gate Inn. 100 N. 200 West; (435) 867-0603; www.theirongateinn.com. Within a short distance of the Iron Gate Inn, the gates of Cedar Breaks National Monument, Zion and Bryce Canyon National Parks, and many other fabulous places wait to welcome you. Originally built in 1897, this newly renovated and richly decorated house emanates pure elegance and comfort. One of the renovations that you will enjoy most is the beautifully landscaped yard. Each room of the Iron Gate Inn has a king-size bed and private bath. Your breakfast will be a variety of wonderfully rich and succulent foods, baked fresh daily. No worries if you have food allergies or restrictions; just give them more than 48 hours notice and they will try to accommodate you. With such an unparalleled feel of ease and quiet, you may opt to just stay in. $$

Storybook Cottage. 218 S. 100 West; (435) 586-8057 or (866) 586-8057; www.story bookbnb.com. Step inside your own storybook, just like you imagined when you were a kid. The Storybook Cottage has the charm of the 1920s but with modern amenities, and it sits on a magnificent tree-lined street just blocks away from the Utah Shakespeare Festival in the center of town. After a restful night's sleep you will be thrilled to awaken to the smells of a full gourmet breakfast. Once the aroma reaches your room, nothing could possibly keep you in bed. $$

day trip 04

south

>>> **the gods' secret hiding spot:**
zion national park

Zion National Park has been said to be the "most beautiful place in America." Utah's oldest national park is home to deep canyons, immense cliffs, and monoliths colored in stunning red rock. This place is truly magnificent and is enjoyed by so many different people with so many different interests. From hikers to backpackers to those who enjoy a scenic drive, Zion has a little something for everyone.

Zion National Park was originally declared a national monument in 1909 when President William Howard Taft dedicated 15,000 acres as the Mukuntuweap National Monument. In 1918 the name was changed to Zion National Monument, and then in November of 1919 the federal government upgraded the area to a national park. The region known as Zion National Park was called "Zion" after the heavenly city in the Bible by the early Latter-day Saint, or "Mormon," settlers. Many of the canyons, trails, and formations were given Biblical names by these early settlers, such as Kolob Canyon and Angel's Landing. Zion National Park now sees more than 1,000,000 visitors per year who come to partake in its beauty.

Because of the number of visitors each year to Zion National Park, the Zion Canyon Scenic Drive is not open to private vehicles from Apr through Oct. However, a free shuttle is available then and private vehicles are allowed on all other roads year-round and on the Zion Canyon Scenic Drive from Nov through Mar. There are 2 shuttles that make loops; one circles through the park and the other through the town of Springdale. The Springdale shuttle will take you to the park's entrance. From Apr through Oct, the parking lot in Zion usually fills up by 10 a.m. Look for blue PARK AND RIDE signs in the town of Springdale. The

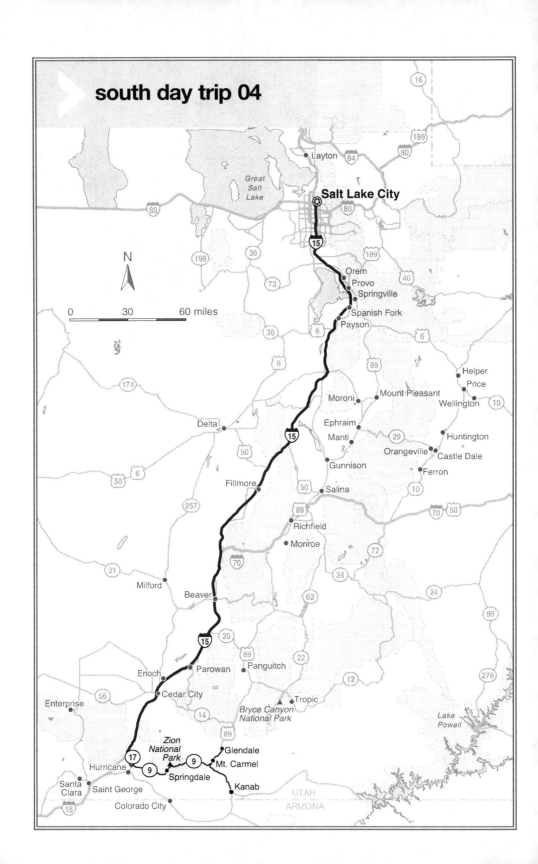

south day trip 04

shuttle runs Apr through Oct from dawn to dusk. Shuttles are free and wheelchair accessible. No pets are allowed on the shuttles.

To help maintain the beauty and majesty of the park, you must pay an entrance fee, which is good for 7 consecutive days. The fees are $25 for each private vehicle (up to 14 people); $12 for each motorcycle (1 person) and $12 more for additional passengers up to $25; and $12 per person for those not in vehicles (15 and under are free). There are other fees such as special-use permits and backcountry permits, for any overnight activity or canyoneering trails, and campground fees. Check the website or call for more information.

getting there

From Salt Lake City, travel south on I-15 for 280 miles. Take exit 27 and merge onto UT 17. Continue south on UT 17 for 6 miles and turn left at UT 9/500 North. Follow UT 9 for 19.5 miles into Springdale and Zion National Park.

where to go

Zion National Park. Springdale, Utah; (435) 772-3256; www.nps.gov/zion. Zion offers a variety of pursuits such as backcountry activities, biking, camping, horseback riding, and sightseeing. The most popular activities are hiking and canyoneering.

Hiking. Hiking opportunities are available to all ages and abilities, with some of the lower trails being wheelchair accessible. Because there are so many trails to choose from, here is a small sample of the more popular trails:

Easy:

- **Watchman Trail.** This trail is good to hike in the morning or evening or during the winter season because it is fully exposed to the sun. Along this trail you will see some magnificent formations such as the West Temple, the Beehive, and Watchman Spire, to name a few. Be sure to use caution, especially with young children, because of steep drop-offs and unstable cliffs. (2.8 miles round-trip)

- **Lower Emerald Pool.** Walk your way through cottonwoods and other riverside plants as you head to a stunning canyon refuge. This trail winds through Zion's spectacular scenery to the Lower Emerald Pool, where you can cool down and relax. From here you can loop back down to the trailhead or continue to the Middle and Upper Emerald Pools. The middle pools and upper pools are for the moderate-level hiker. (1.2 miles round-trip)

Moderate:

- **Middle and Upper Emerald Pools.** After rejuvenating at the Lower Emerald Pool, continue your hike up to the splendor of Middle Emerald Pool, which gives the hiker breathtaking views of some amazing formations such as the Cathedral and Red Arch

Mountains. From here you can continue your hike up to the Upper Emerald Pool or make a loop back down. For those who continue to the upper pools, your effort will be rewarded. At the Upper Emerald Pool you will take pleasure in the magnificence of Zion Canyon, and during runoff months, strong and powerful waterfalls. (2 miles round-trip to middle pool; 3 miles round-trip to upper pool)

- **Sand Bench Loop.** The Sand Bench is a colossal earthen shelf created by an ancient landslide. The trail is extremely sandy, but the scenery is amazing. Pack your food for a picnic at the end of the loop, where you can look down into the mouth of Zion Canyon. This is also a horseback trail, so watch for horse waste along the way. (3.5 miles round-trip)

Strenuous:

- **Kolob Arch.** There are 2 different ways to reach the famous Kolob Arch, the second largest arch in the world. The most popular is to descend from the Kolob Canyon Road parking lot at Lee Pass. You can also start at the Hop Valley trailhead. From either place, the distance is the same. The arch is not as stunning as other arches, but still worth the hike. (14 miles round-trip)

- **The Narrows.** The most popular hike in Zion National Park is The Narrows. Plan on getting wet, as the Virgin River is the trail. Begin at the Temple of Sinawava, where the trail is paved for about a mile, and then you continue up the river. For the full 16-mile hike, start at Chamberlain Ranch (top) and hike down to the Temple of Sinawava. If you are planning to hike the entire Narrows, a permit that can be obtained from any Zion National Park visitor center is required. (Up to 16 miles)

Technical:
Permits are required for the following hikes, obtainable from any visitor center in the park.

- **The Subway.** On this journey you will be hiking, climbing, descending, and swimming your way to reach the Subway. The Subway gets it name from canyon walls that arch over a small but amazing waterfall and create a tunnel. You will also be able to see dinosaur tracks from the Jurassic period. *Warning:* Only attempt this canyon if you are hiking with an experienced canyoneer. (9.5 miles)

- **Orderville Gulch.** This hike will take you through canyons that are steeper and narrower than even the famous Narrows. You will find yourself in some areas where the walls of the canyon are only 10 feet apart. This is a great place to learn canyoneering because of its relatively few technical spots in the canyon. Plan on getting wet on this adventure, as you will be wading and swimming. The views will be worth your effort. (11 miles one way)

If it rains while you're visiting Zion, do not fret! **Zion National Park is amazing on a rainy day.** *Take time to ride through the park. The large sandstone cliffs turn into waterfalls that normally are nonexistent on dry days. It will be worth your time. (Be careful not to get caught in a slot canyon during a rainstorm; water moves fast and furious into these canyons.)*

Other Activities in Zion:

- **Biking.** The Pa'rus Trail (3.5 miles long) is the only established bike trail in Zion National Park, but thanks to the shuttle the roads in Zion have become more popular. However, keep in mind that cyclists are not allowed through the Zion–Mt. Carmel Tunnel. Many bicyclists ride the shuttle to the top of Zion Canyon and ride the Scenic Drive downhill and then along the Pa'rus Trail.

- **Camping.** (877) 444-6777. (Campground fees are in addition to the entrance fee.) Zion National Park has 2 developed campgrounds and a primitive campground right inside the park. The **Watchman Campground** is developed and open year-round, with many sites to choose from, including RV sites. Prices depend on the site you want, so call for reservations and more information. The **South Campground** is another developed campground and is open from Mar through Oct. Sites are available on a first-come, first-serve basis. There are no hookups or showers at this campground. There is a $16-a-night fee to camp at the South Campground. **Lava Point Campground** is undeveloped and open June through Oct. There are no bathrooms at this campground, and no reservations are required. There is no fee to camp at Lava Point Campground.

- **Canyon trail rides.** (435) 679-8665; www.canyonrides.com. A 1-hour trip costs $40 per person, and a half-day trip costs $75 per person.

- **Horseback riding.** See the wonders of Zion and the surrounding area on horseback. There are a number of vendors that provide horseback tours in and out of the park. One suggestion is:

   Zion Mountain Resort. (866) 648-2555; www.zmr.com. A 1-hour trip costs $35 per person. (Located outside the park, on the east side.)

Best Friends Animal Sanctuary. 5001 Angel Canyon Rd., Kanab (5 miles north of Kanab); (435) 644-2001, ext. 4537; www.bestfriends.org. Best Friends Animal Sanctuary is the largest sanctuary for abused animals in the nation. According to the sanctuary, on any given day they care for 1,700 animals. The shelter provides a place for animals to receive

mystic river trout fishing pond

*There are 2 entrances to Zion National Park. If you choose the east entrance, take a few moments and catch the fish of your dreams. **Mystic River Trout Fishing Pond** is a fisherman's dream. Whether you are an experienced fly fisherman or have never fished in your life, you need to stop and see the beautiful ponds and fish just waiting to be caught. There is a trophy pond, which is catch-and-release only and is $50 per hour. Pull in the big ones: 9 to 10 pounders. The other pond allows either catch-and-release at $30 per hour, or catch-and-eat, which is $12 per pound plus $9 per plate for all the other fixin's. No license is required; they supply the poles and can provide fly rod lessons as well. The pond is located just north of Glendale on US 89 between Zion and Bryce Canyon. Spend the day at the park, enjoy caching dinner, and let the cooks at Mystic River clean, cook, and serve you the freshest trout you've ever had. Open 9 a.m. to dusk. Call and verify days and pricing, as they are subject to change; (435) 648-2823.*

special care and love while waiting for adoption. Come visit and take a 1½ hour guided tour of this refuge as you wind through the splendid beauty of Angel Canyon.

Bumbleberry Playhouse. 97 Bumbleberry Lane, Springdale; (435) 772-3224 or (800) 828-1534; www.bumbleberry.com. Although this theater has had many names, the variety of fun had while visiting this little playhouse hasn't changed a bit. Enjoy live entertainment from local artists after a day in the outdoors to add to the memories you have made in Springdale. At Christmastime enjoy Christmas concerts and a chance to see Santa. Call for more information and ticket prices.

Coral Pink Sand Dunes State Park. Near Kanab, 12 miles southwest of US 89; (435) 648-2800 or (800) 322-3770; www.utah.com/stateparks/coral_pink.htm. Located just southeast of Zion National Park, the Coral Pink Sand Dunes offer incredible sights for photographers and outdoor enthusiasts as well. The coral-colored sand is surrounded by southern Utah's red rocks and dark green forests. With 1,000 acres of trails, the Coral Pink Sand Dunes are an off-road "playground." You will also find great trails for hiking. For the many children and those adults who are young at heart and love to play in the sand, camping is also available. From Zion's east exit, take UT 9 to Mt. Carmel Junction and turn left (south) onto US 89. After about 6 miles, watch for the CORAL PINK STATE PARK signs. Turn right onto Yellowjacket Road and follow it to the park. The day use fee is $5; Camping costs $14 a night.

Kanab "Little Hollywood." Kanab is just 40 miles southeast of Zion National Park. From the east park exit, follow UT 9 to Mt. Carmel Junction. Turn right (south) onto US 89 and follow it into Kanab. Kanab was given the nickname "Little Hollywood" because of the many TV shows and movies (mostly westerns) that were filmed in and around the town. The stunning red rocks, coral pink sands, volcanic craters, and stately mountains make it the perfect setting for movies such as *The Outlaw Josey Wales, She Wore a Yellow Ribbon,* and *MacKenna's Gold,* to name a few. The TV show *Gunsmoke* was filmed in nearby Paria Canyon. Kanab also has an Old Town Movie Set that visitors can walk through to get a feel for old western towns. Be sure to stop at the Perry Lodge right on Main Street, where many actors and actress stayed while filming shows.

Zion Canyon is also close to **Bryce Canyon National Park, Lake Powell, Grand Staircase-Escalante National Monument,** and **The Grand Canyon** (Arizona).

where to shop

Apple Hollow Artist Co-op. 75 N. Main St., Glendale; (435) 648-3048; www.visiteastzion .info/apple. Many different artists, such as painters, jewelry crafters, potters, and handcrafters, contribute to the charm and high-quality souvenirs that await you here. You will find unique gifts that are sure to please yourself or someone at home.

Crystals & Creatures. 801 Zion Park Blvd., Springdale; (435) 772-0577; www.crystals-creatures.com. Here you will find just what the names suggests: crystals, minerals, and jewelry. You can also get carved animals and walking sticks. For your mind and body, they have music, art, and collectibles, as well as creams and essential oils.

DeZion Gallery. 1501 Zion Park Blvd., Springdale; (435) 772-6888; www.deziongallery .com. This gallery is known as the "Gallery for Locals." The artwork here is ever-changing because they feature creations from local and regional artists. Browse their selection of paintings, mosaics, and glasswork. You will also find homemade drums, native flutes, pottery, gourds, paper, and jewelry.

Regalo. 932 Zion Park Blvd., Springdale; (435) 772-0616. If you are looking for recycled or Earth-friendly items, this shop is for you. They specialize in beads, Mexican folk art, cards, and jewelry.

Springdale Candy Company. 855A Zion Park Blvd., Springdale; (435) 772-0485; www .springdalecandycompany.com. Opened in 2008, this "sweet" candy store is dedicated to making the best homemade chocolates and confections, such as hand-dipped chocolates, divinity, fudge, and peanut brittle. Everyone will love the traditional favorites like saltwater taffy, gummies, and jelly beans in a variety of flavors. They also have the latest fun in kid's candy. Stop here before starting your day in Zion and come back for a delicious "end of the day" treat! Your taste buds will thank you!

Thunderbird Gift Shop. Mt. Carmel Junction; (435) 648-2203. Located east of Zion National Park at the junction of UT 9 and US 89, this shop provides an eclectic array of southwestern souvenirs. Here you will find Native American rugs, jewelry, pottery, and dolls. Also look over their collection of rocks for sale.

Zion Lodge Gift Shop. Zion National Park; (435) 772-7700; www.zionlodge.com. The only lodge in Zion National Park provides a gift shop for guests as well as tourists. Pick from a variety of items to help you remember the remarkable landscape and special sites that Zion provides. You can also find Native American and southwestern souvenirs such as pottery, jewelry, and artwork.

where to eat

Blue Belly Grill. North Fork Road, Mt. Carmel (Zion Ponderosa Ranch Resort); (800) 293-5444; www.bluebellygrill.com. Don't let the grill in the name fool you—the food here is gourmet. Satisfy your palate with pork, chicken, steak, filet mignon, or fish. The food will please you and the atmosphere will delight you. Reservations recommended. Open May through Sept. $$

Buffalo Bistro. US 89, Glendale; (435) 648-2778; www.buffalobistro.net. For a truly unique western meal, this restaurant is a must. To start out, try an appetizer such as Rabbit Rattlesnake Sausage or Rocky Mountain oysters (yes, the real thing). The dinner menu is just as unique with a Rocky Mountain oyster dinner ("no bull") or Half Rabbit dinner. But, no worries, if you want a traditional meal, they have that too! Closed Tues and Wed, open 4 p.m. "'til I pass out." $$

Castle Dome Cafe. Zion Lodge, Zion National Park; (435) 772-7760 (open seasonally); www.zionlodge.com. If you're in a hurry but want a delicious meal, then Castle Dome Cafe is for you. During the peak season, Castle Dome Cafe is open for all 3 meals. In the morning grab your coffee or espresso and cinnamon roll, or other continental breakfast items, and go. Later in the day, enjoy such things as a burger or hot dog, fries, or other quick foods to fill your belly and get you on your way—or cool down with some soft-serve ice cream. $

Historic Pioneer Restaurant. 838 Zion Park Blvd., Springdale; (435) 772-3009; www.historicpioneerrestaurant.com. Famous for their breakfast, homemade bread, and prime rib, this restaurant will satisfy your appetite for good food. Start off with a variety of appetizers and then move on to a hearty meal of steak, shrimp, chicken, or fish. Top it all off with a delicious homemade pie. Prime rib is served Fri and Sat only. $$

Red Rock Grill. Zion Lodge, Zion National Park; (435) 772-7760; www.zionlodge.com. Enjoy breakfast, lunch, or dinner surrounded by the beauty of Zion National Park. Red Rock Grill is a full-service dining room that offers a breakfast menu sure to please everyone. For dinner choose from an array of menu items ranging from mouthwatering pasta dishes to different kinds of succulent fish. Or, if your appetite is on the lighter side, they have salads or a soup and salad combination to choose from. Red Rock Grill is open year-round, with a seasonal open-air terrace. Dinner reservations are required. $$

Sol Foods Cafe. 95 Zion Park Blvd., Springdale; (435) 772-0277; www.solfoods.com. Enjoy your meal as you sit in the only outdoor dining on the banks of the Virgin River and appreciate the views of Zion National Park. Sol Foods Cafe serves delicious sandwiches or wraps, or you can try one of their specialties, such as a buffalo burger, fish-and-chips, or the vegetarian burger. Top off your meal with ice cream, a milk shake, or baked goods. $

Wildcat Willies Ranch Grill Saloon. 879 Zion Park Blvd., Springdale; (435) 772-0115; www.wildcatwillies.com. This "Old Wild West" restaurant offers breakfast, lunch, and dinner. You will not go away hungry from this place. The menu offers quite a variety to satisfy even the pickiest eater, from ribs or steak, to chicken, pork, or fish. Choose from an assortment of salads, pasta dishes, or pizzas. They even have a menu for the "little buckaroos" in your party. If you have room, try one of their "lip-smacking" desserts. $$

where to stay

East Entrance:

Zion Lodge. Zion National Park; (435) 772-7700; toll-free within the US, (888) 297-2757; outside the US, (303) 297-2757; www.zionlodge.com. Zion Lodge is the only in-park accommodation at Zion National Park. This lodge offers rustic cabins with 2 double beds, full bath, gas log fireplace, and a private porch. The lodge also offers suites, which include a sitting room with a couch that folds out to a queen-size bed, a wet bar, a small refrigerator, and sink and faucet. A separate sleeping room comes with a king-size bed. Motel rooms are available as well, and most rooms come with 2 queen-size beds (some have 1 king-size bed), a full bath, and a private porch or balcony. While at the lodge you can dine in the dining room of Red Rock Grill (reservations required) or enjoy the beauty of the park by eating outdoors at the seasonal Castle Dome Cafe. $$$

Zion Mountain Ranch. East UT 9, Zion National Park; (866) 648-2555; www.zmr.com. Just 3 minutes from the east entrance to Zion National Park, you will find an oasis from the hustle and bustle of life at this unique ranch that is home to a roaming herd of buffalo. Enjoy the beauty and majesty of Zion National Park and stay in cabins that will feel like your home away from home. Unwind in a spacious yet comfy cabin or cabin suite. Each cabin and cabin suite comes with a king-size bed, private bathroom, heating and air-conditioning, gas fireplace, TV with satellite, DVD player, refrigerator, microwave, and coffeemaker. Suites have jetted tubs and a few come with kitchenettes. Cabins $$–$$$; cabin suites $$$

Zion Ponderosa Ranch Resort. North Fork Road, Mt. Carmel; (435) 648-2700 or (800) 293-5444; www.zionponderosa.com. Spend a day exploring Zion National Park or spend your time at the Ranch Resort. This place has everything to make your stay exciting and adventurous.

If you feel like roughing it, you can bring your own tent or rent one (sleeps 5 to 6), and sleep at one of their tent camping sites. All campsites include wireless Internet, access to their open-use activities, hot showers in the shower house, a coin-operated laundry, and picnic table and grill. Campsites cost $10 a person a night; tent rental costs $20 a night.

If you want to camp, but not in a tent, RV sites are available. Enjoy the great outdoors with roomy back-in sites and room for multiple slides. Relax while surrounded by pinion pines and Utah junipers with Zion National Park in the background. Each site includes access to their open-use activities, wireless Internet, 30- and 50-amp service, full hookups, coin-operated laundry room and shower house, and a grill and picnic table. The cost is $47 per night.

If camping is not what you have in mind for your vacation, maybe a cabin will do. Zion Ponderosa has many cabins that will make your stay relaxing yet still give you that outdoorsy feeling. Each Cowboy Cabin sleeps up to 6, with comfortable beds, a front porch, access to the shower house, and use of other resort facilities. $

"Roughing it" with style has never been easier when you stay in one of the cabin suites that Zion Ponderosa Ranch offers. These cabins come with a private bedroom, full bathroom, wet bar, a front room with a fold-out couch, air-conditioning, front porch, and, in a few, a fireplace. Each cabin suite sleeps up to 6 people. $$$

A special lodging policy is available during peak season only: a minimum of 1 activity voucher purchase per person is required ($15 per voucher). For larger groups, vacation homes are available. Call or visit www.zionponderosa.com for more information.

Springdale Entrance:

Bumbleberry Inn. 97 Bumbleberry Lane, Springdale; (435) 772-3224 or (800) 828-1534; www.bumbleberry.com. This quaint, family-owned and -operated inn offers modern rooms at an affordable price. Get away from the chaos of city life and enjoy some quiet, beautiful scenery. Bumbleberry Inn is nestled at the mouth of Zion National Park. Every room has a mini-fridge, microwave, and a private balcony or patio. Also enjoy television with satellite. You can choose either a room with 2 queen-size beds and a private bathroom with a shower/bath combination and a vanity area, or a room with 1 queen bed and a private bathroom with a shower. Or enjoy a mini-suite, with 1 queen bed and either a jetted tub or a fireplace. Cool down and relax in the outdoor swimming pool, which has an adjacent kids' pool. The Zion National Park shuttle stops here, so you can leave your car. While staying here, catch a play at the Bumbleberry Playhouse and don't forget to try a slice of delicious bumbleberry pie at the bakery—you'll be glad you did! $–$$

Canyon Vista Bed & Breakfast. 2175 Zion Park Blvd., Springdale; (435) 772-3801; www.canyonvistabandb.com. Your visit to Zion National Park will be more memorable staying at this fun bed-and-breakfast, where each room has a different Native American name.

Whether staying in the Sinewava, Kinesava, Pa'rus, or Mukuntuweap room, you will enjoy a uniquely different style of decor, but will receive the same level of comfort. Each room has its own private bath with a tub/shower combination or jetted tub/shower combination. Relax while watching TV with satellite or surf the web with wireless Internet access. Rooms come with a kitchenette that has a compact microwave, sink, coffeemaker, dishware, and dining area. Choose from either an in-room continental breakfast or get a breakfast voucher redeemable at local restaurants, with breakfast service from 6:30 to 11 a.m. (A 2-night minimum stay is required from Memorial Day through Nov 14; call within 2 weeks of your stay if you only need 1 night.) $$

Red Rock Inn B&B Cottages. 998 Zion Park Blvd., Springdale; (435) 772-3139; www .redrockinn.com. Enjoy the splendor of Zion National Park while staying in a bed-and-breakfast cottage. Each cottage is uniquely decorated to fit the majestic landscape that surrounds it while offering relaxation and leisure. For a more romantic getaway, try the cottage suite, which includes a queen-size brass bed and 2 bathrooms, a sitting room, and an outdoor Jacuzzi spa on the private patio. Each cottage receives a full hot breakfast delivered to your door in a wicker basket. $$

Zion Canyon Bed & Breakfast. 101 Kokopelli Circle, Springdale; (435)772-9466; www .zioncanyonbandb.com. Zion Canyon Bed & Breakfast is set back to offer quiet serenity, yet it's within walking distance to the main part of Springdale for shopping, restaurants, and the shuttle into Zion National Park. Each room is decorated differently, but with the same ambience of the red rocks that surround it. This place will provide a retreat whether you're here to hike or sightsee, or for rest and relaxation. No matter what room you choose, you will be enjoying a king-size or queen-size bed, with a pillow-top mattress, a private bathroom, a flat-screen TV with cable, wireless Internet access, and spectacular views. In the morning you will be treated to a delicious 2-course breakfast in their dining room. (Children 10 and older welcome.) $$–$$$

southwest

day trip 01

southwest

digging to china:
bingham canyon

High above the valley floor sits a mammoth hole. Take a peek over the edge of the overlook and you will begin to get a sense for just how massive this excavation is. It is, in fact, the largest man-made excavation on Earth.

The Kennecott Copper Mine is an open-pit mining operation, with its main purpose to mine for porphyry copper. Two brothers first discovered copper ore in the canyon in 1848, but it wasn't until 1863 that extraction actually began. The terrain was so rugged that it took several years for the large-scale production to finally become successful. Once a railroad was established, the mining went full force; little towns were built on these mountains, and many jobs were formed. The mine has been in full production since 1906, resulting in a pit nearly a mile deep and 2.5 miles wide, covering over 1,900 acres. In 1966 Bingham Canyon Open Pit Mine was named a National Historic Landmark. To date, the Kennecott Mine has produced over 18.7 million tons of copper, more than any mine in history. One of the most amazing facts of this significant mine is that it is so big, it can be seen by astronauts on the space shuttle as they pass over the United States.

getting there

From Salt Lake City, travel south on I-15 to 10600 South, exit 297. Follow SR 48 west to SR 111. Turn left onto SR 111 and travel south until you reach the visitor center on your right.

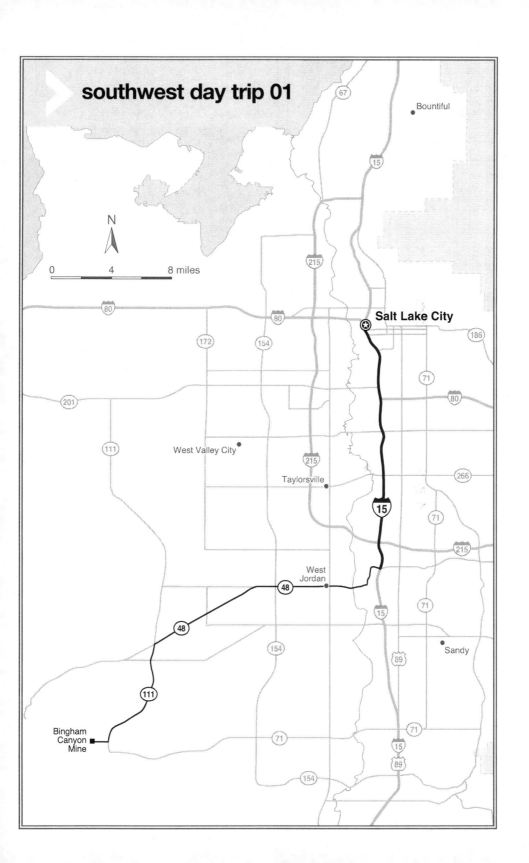

southwest day trip 01

where to go

Bingham Canyon Mine Visitor Center. 8400 W. 12300 South, SR 111; (801) 252-3234; www.kennecot.com. Open from Apr 1 to Oct 31 7 days a week, from 8 a.m. to 8 p.m. To visit the mine, a small donation of $5 for passenger vehicles is asked for, and all proceeds are donated to local charities. Here you can learn about the history of the mine and many little-known facts about mining and mineral ore. You can also view the mine from the overlook within the visitor center. Watch in amazement as trucks that look like small toy vehicles carry ore to the crusher. These tiny-looking trucks aren't small at all—they are 23 feet tall. (The drivers' seats are 18 feet above the ground—that's 2 stories high!) They have the ability to carry 240 to 360 tons of copper ore at a time, which is then reduced into chunks the size of soccer balls and loaded onto a 5-mile conveyor belt. As you watch the work, a recorded narrative describes the operations of the mine. Inside the visitor center, family members can have some hands-on experiences, including the opportunity to look at rocks and mineral samples. You will also learn the many uses of copper in everyday life.

Over 150,000 tons of copper is produced here every day, proving Bingham Mine to be of the utmost importance to Utah's economy and the world's industries. A day at the mine can be awe inspiring and extremely educational. The thought of digging to China will take on a whole new meaning. The view of the valley from atop is also not to be missed.

day trip 02

southwest

the happy lake:
utah lake

This lake is one of the largest freshwater lakes west of the Mississippi River. Come for the day and enjoy the fishing, camping, and boating opportunities Utah Lake provides.

getting there

From Salt Lake City, drive south on I-15 to the Provo Center Street exit. Turn right and follow the signs to the state park.

where to go

Utah Lake State Park. 4400 W. Center St., Provo (5 miles west of Provo), just off I-15; (801) 375-0731; www.utah.com/stateparks/utah_lake. If you are a fishermen, you can enjoy a huge variety of fish, including catfish, walleye, white bass, black bass, and panfish. If fishing isn't what you are after, you can enjoy the 96,000-acre lake for sailboating, powerboating, or canoeing; with a 4-boat launching ramp and a 30-acre marina, room isn't a problem. Campers can enjoy modern restrooms, 71 campsites, bathing facilities, and RV amenities. There are also several accommodations for the disabled.

Utah Lake Festival. This annual event is an exciting time for visitors to enjoy free food, fishing, and lots of fun! Amateur fishermen will enjoy having an expert instructor to help give hands-on lessons. Events may change from year to year; however, the main goal will remain

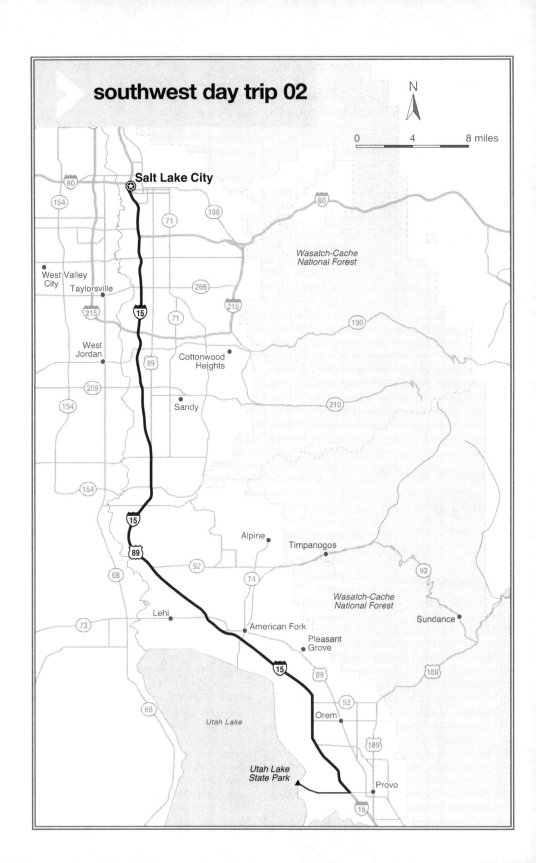

the same: to instill a love of the lake through education and experience. Free tours of the lake, canoeing workshops, and a special waterskiing show will keep guests entertained all day while educating them on the importance of Utah Lake.

day trip 03

southwest

dunes & dinos:
delta

The word *delta* means "fertile area near a river's mouth." Here in this mostly arid desert, the Sevier River was diverted into Delta, and reservoirs give life to this onetime railroad facility they once called Akin. If you ask the old timers, they might argue that the name of the town is either Melville or Burtner, as this town has gone by all of these names in years gone by. After many attempts to give the town a name it could live with, the town decided to have a contest. In 1911 Burtner was incorporated and the name Delta became official.

The area has quite a history and has contributed much to the nation. It is the location of the Topaz Relocation Camp, where Japanese-Americans were held after the attack on Pearl Harbor. It is also the site of one of the few beryllium mines in the world. This is a vital metal used in the military, aerospace, and medical industries, and though it is mined 50 miles from Delta, the mill and finishing facility is a major contributor to the economy.

Delta is not a big place, and the people who live here probably would just as well keep it that way. It has that Mayberry, small-town feeling where you know what trouble your child got into before he walks in the front door—a place where the whole town turns out for the Christmas parade. Enjoy a walk around town as you visit some of the day trips we found there.

getting there

From Salt Lake City, head south on I-15 for 62 miles and take exit 244 and merge onto US 6. Stay on US 6 for 71.1 miles and arrive at Delta.

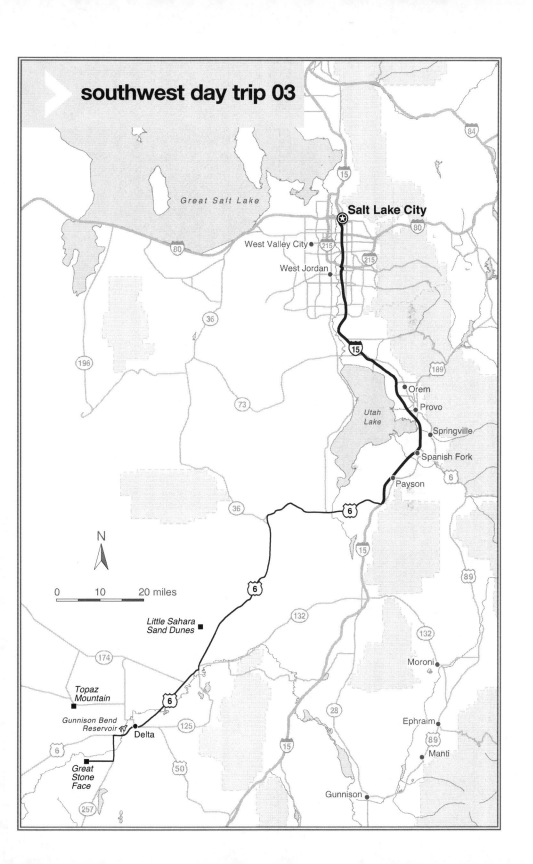

where to go

The Bug House. 350 E. 300 South, Delta; (435) 864-2402; www.info@thebughouse.net. Delta is prime rock-hunting country, and The Bug House offers visitors the opportunity to purchase and view various fossils and other products. They carry educational kits filled with rocks, fossils, and various minerals. Other products include dugway geodes and septarian nodules. Day tours are available to different rock and fossil locations in the West Desert.

Crystal Peak. From Delta, head west on US 6/US 50. The road will head straight for 48 miles, then will bend in the mountains at Skull Rock Pass. At this point look for a well-graded dirt road to the left, around 1 mile from the road bend. Take this road, Tule Valley Road, and begin to head south to where the road ends at a T intersection after 20.5 miles. Go right at this intersection and head west, on Crystal Peak Road. You will be able to see the peak from this point. Drive another 11 miles on Crystal Peak Road. Park your car as close as you can get, and begin your hike on the east side of the peak. Crystal Peak is unique, formed 34 million years ago, and composed of white volcanic rock. This peak predates the Great Basin Desert with rock that is filled with holes, where pumice once lived. Hiking Crystal Peak doesn't take long, but be sure to use the route mentioned because the other sides are much steeper and can be a dangerous to hike, as the rock is brittle and breaks off easily.

Great Basin Historical Society Museum. 328 W. 100 North, Delta; (435) 864-5013; www.greatbasin@hubwest.com. This museum features many exhibits and displays about West Millard history. Many artifacts of early settlers and quite an extensive archive of photos and documents about the surrounding area are housed here. An exhibit about the World War II Topaz Relocation Center, located a mere 16 miles from Delta, is displayed at the museum. This camp held more than 8,300 internees, mostly from the San Francisco Bay area, from 1942 to 1946. The original building from this camp is located at the museum site. Exhibits of many fossils, geodes, and other ores found in the area are also on display and will please even the most hardcore rock hound.

Little Sahara. Located approximately 115 miles from Salt Lake City. From Nephi, 31 miles west via SR 132 and CR 1812; from Eureka, 18 miles south on US 6; from Delta, 34 miles north on US 6, 4 miles west of Jericho Junction. To get to the **Little Sahara Visitor Center** (435-433-5960), use the main road (US 6) from Provo. The entrance road to the recreation area leaves US 6 near Jericho. After a few miles it passes the visitor center. By the means of a huge sand source and strong winds, Little Sahara was created. Most of the sand was deposited by the Sevier River, which once flowed into the ancient Lake Bonneville over 15,000 years ago. As the lake receded, winds picked up loose sand and deposited the particles in the ultimate creation of a 124-square-mile system of giant sand dunes (see sidebar).

Great Stone Face. From Delta travel approximately 5 miles on US 6/US 50 to SR 257. From SR 257, travel for 6.1 miles to the Great Stone Face turnoff. Parking is located after another 5.8 miles. This natural rock formation is also known as the Guardian of Deseret. The

rockwell outstanding natural area

Some people like to experience the quiet side of the dunes at the Rockwell Out-standing Natural Area in Little Sahara. This vehicle-free zone has a wide array of plants, including an extremely rare species of saltbush. It is also a great place to see the variety of animals that exist in this area. Mule deer, antelope, birds, and many reptiles call this place home. If you're a rider, there are many options in this ATV, dune buggy, 60,000-acre paradise filled with sand dunes, trails, and sagebrush flats.

Some suggestions:

Sand Mountain. *This huge wall of sand climbs approximately 700 feet and pro-vides the ultimate challenge to riders and their machines.*

White Sand Dunes. *This spot is on the north end of the recreation area and attracts riders of all levels. It's very accessible and has hundreds of riding bowls.*

Dunes southwest of Black Mountain. *This is a great place for beginners to play because of the low-lying dunes. It tends to be less crowded here.*

Black Mountain. *A system of dirt trails wind up and around this peak. It offers fan-tastic trail rides for almost all off-road vehicles.*

Mormon pioneers came across this rock after traveling hundreds of miles by handcart to settle in the western wilderness. Just before the parking area, there are also the Great Stone Face Petroglyphs. It is not known what the symbols mean, but some believe it is an agree-ment of dividing water and hunting privileges among the Indians on the lower Sevier River.

Gunnison Bend Reservoir. From Delta, travel west on Main Street, cross the overpass, and take the road to Sutherland. Turn left at 3000 West and travel 2 miles south. Officially developed in 1895 by the pioneers as a necessary reservoir for farmers to use to water their crops during the hot summer months, this dam now provides an excellent place for water sports and fishing, and a small area for beach bathers. Most of the dam shoreline is privately owned; however, there is a boat dock and beach area at Gunderson Bend Park. Guests will enjoy picnic tables, a covered pavilion, and restrooms (which make the stay even better). A peninsula of land prevents large waves and the water remains quite warm due to its shallow depths. For the fishermen, bass, catfish, yellow perch, carp, bluegill, and walleye could possibly be on the menu!

Topaz Mountain. Located about 40 miles west of Delta, at the southern end of the Thomas Mountain Range. Topaz is Utah's state gem and is considered a semiprecious stone. These crystals are formed in the cavities of Topaz Mountain rhyolit, which is a volcanic rock that erupted here over 6 million years ago. The area is very hot and dry and there are no amenities for visitors, so make sure to bring lots of water and food. There is plenty of open space, so camping is allowed. It's not a bad idea to bring umbrellas to provide shade since there are not many trees to give you relief from the hot summer sun. Topaz sediments are fragile but can be found, even though many say the mountain has been picked over. With the correct tools and a little hard work, rock hounders will find some beautiful sherry-colored topaz! Clear topaz can also be found, which results from radiation and heat from the sun. A hammer, screwdriver, and screen are suggested tools. If you screen in dirt washes and around vegetation, you should easily end up with several pieces of topaz. Good luck and happy hunting!

U-DIG Fossils. Office (which is not located at the quarry site): 350 E. 300 South, Delta; (435) 864-3638; www.u-digfossils.com. Located 52 miles west from Delta, near Antelope Springs. From Delta travel 32 miles west on US 6/US 50. At the Long Ridge Reservoir sign, between mile markers 56 and 57, turn right. At this intersection, there is a U-DIG FOSSILS sign. Travel another 20 miles on a maintained gravel road to reach the U-DIG Quarry. All types of vehicles can travel to this site; having tools on hand to change a tire is a good idea, though, considering it is a dirt road. RVs are welcome but camping is not allowed. The nearest gas and food services are located in Delta.

This wonderful quarry is a family-run business that houses one of the richest trilobite deposits in the world. A trilobite is an invertebrate marine life form that lived more than 500 million years ago. They are very popular fossil finds because they are often preserved perfectly. They are found in limestone shale, a beautiful black-looking rock. Here you will use picks to split apart the flat sheets of shale—easily done, as the shale splits without difficulty. U-DIG staff members extract and expose new rock regularly; however, you may remove your own fresh rock if desired. Guests are able to dig for their own fossil trilobites on any location within the quarry and are allowed to keep their treasures. Most visitors will find 10 to 20 trilobites. If you are having trouble, the U-DIG personnel can help you find the best areas to dig. It is recommended to bring a pair of gloves, sturdy shoes, safety glasses, a light jacket, food, and plenty of water!

where to eat

Loft Steakhouse. 411 E. Main St.; (435) 864-4223. This is the place to go for steak in Delta. The friendly and personable staff will treat you with homemade soups and incredible desserts. It's right on Main Street, so it is easy to get to. This is a favorite of the locals and visitors alike. $$

Mi Rancherito Mexican Restaurant. 540 Topaz Blvd.; (435) 864-4245. Located directly across from Days Inn, this eating establishment is a must. Tourists and locals enjoy this authentic Mexican restaurant, where the food is prepared fresh by 2 fantastic chefs. Chips and salsa are complimentary for each table. Some of the favorites include chicken enchiladas and *carne asada*. Try this food and you'll feel like you are in Mexico. *"Olé!"* $$

where to stay

Days Inn. 527 East Topaz Blvd.; (435) 864-3882; www.daysinn.com. This is considered by some an oasis in the desert. Days Inn is a pet-friendly hotel that welcomes guests with an indoor pool, complimentary continental breakfast, and clean rooms. Across the street are a movie theater and bowling alley, so you can relax and enjoy your time in Delta as you try to figure out which sight to see first. $

Camping:

Jericho. This is a great area for larger groups, with its paved parking, 41 picnic tables, and shaded ramadas, and you will feel a bit less like you are camping here. There are flushing toilets, an amphitheater, drinking water, and a fenced sand play area for the kids.

Oasis. This is the most developed campsite in the area. It provides paved pads and ready access to the dunes. There are 114 campsites with drinking water, flushing toilets, and an RV dump station.

Rockwell Natural Area. This protected area is a great spot for backpacking. Black Mountain is the highest of the peaks at 5,828 feet. It provides a sheltered habitat from the desert for the many plants and animals.

Sand Mountain. If you like roughing it a little more, this camping area is more primitive than the other sites. There are only 3 paved parking loops, plus tent spaces and vault toilets, and drinking water is available.

White Sands. This is a very popular campsite that affords easy access to the dunes right at your "doorstep." White Sands provides a 700-foot climbable dune, both by off-road vehicles and by foot. Once on top you get a great view of miles of dunes and can pick out your next climb and adventure. Be careful not to get blown away, by the view and the wind.

west

day trip 01

west

a last inland sea:
the great salt lake

You don't have to drive very far out of Salt Lake City to begin to imagine how barren this land looked when the first settlers came into the valley. The farther west you travel the more the words of those pioneers ring true: "We have traveled fifteen hundred miles to get here, and I would willingly travel a thousand miles farther to get where it looked as though a man could live." (Clara Decker, pioneer)

What many of us don't see at first, however, is an ecosystem that is vast and ready to be explored. Stand long and still on the shore of this, the fourth largest terminal lake on Earth, which covers nearly 1,700 square miles in an average year, or on the immense salt flats where the lake once reached, and you will soon discover a world so unique, so alive that you will want to spend days delving into it.

getting there

Great Salt Lake State Park/Saltair Beach is about 16 miles west of Salt Lake City, along I-80. Take exit 104 and follow the frontage road east to the State Park and Marina.

where to go

The Great Salt Lake. State Marina and Visitor Center; (801) 250-1898; open year-round; entrance fee $2 per vehicle. First of all, your day trip cannot be complete without an evening trip to the lake. The sunsets here are amazing. So plan on an afternoon adventure followed by a breathtaking display of color in the evening sky.

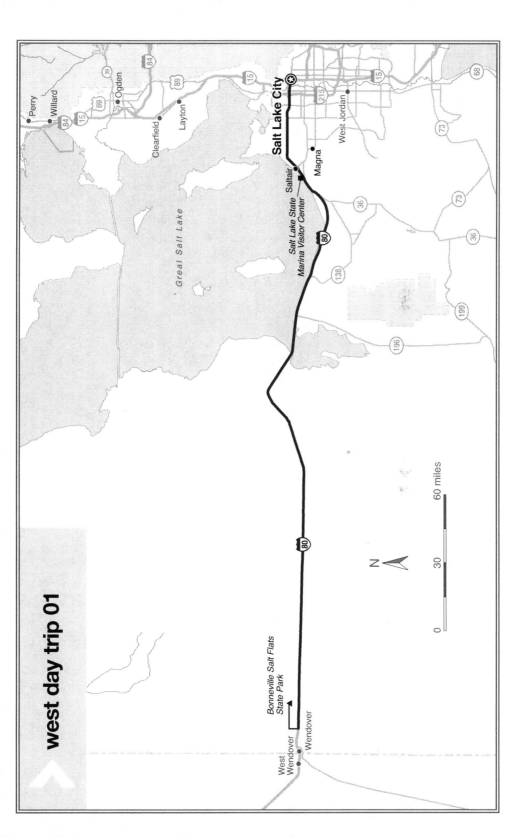

west day trip 01

Salt Lake City

Salt Lake State Marina Visitor Center
Saltair

Magna

West Jordan

Great Salt Lake

Ogden
Willard
Perry
Clearfield
Layton

Bonneville Salt Flats
State Park

West
Wendover

Wendover

N

0   30   60 miles

For those who have always lived in the Salt Lake area, the lake is often thought of as just a lake that can't be used. Besides, with so many incredible freshwater lakes around, why go to a dead one? However, the Great Salt Lake is one of the most visited tourist destinations in Utah. On the south end, you have the marina, visitor center, and the vibrantly rebuilt Saltair (a once thriving resort in the early 1900s), which is the best place to start your excursion. You may encounter the occasional Salt Lake bather. Though bathing in the lake was a popular pastime in its heyday for the mineral benefits, dipping in is not as trendy these days. Still, if you want to test the buoyancy of the water (an average of 12 percent salinity, with some places as high as 27 percent), take the plunge. You can use the showers and bathrooms at the Saltair to freshen up afterward (summer only). If you do venture out, you will find the lake to be very shallow, especially at the south end. The depth averages only ½ to 2 feet, enabling you to go a long way out from the shore. The marina area is great for picnicking, swimming, and watching the abundance of wildlife.

By the way, the Great Salt Lake really isn't dead at all. If you look closely, you will see tiny creatures. If as a child you ever owned or wanted to own a sea monkey, dip your hand in here—there are millions of them. Harvest time for the brine shrimp begins the first of Oct, and over 19 million pounds of the tiny shrimp are harvested each year. That's a lot of shrimp sauce! It is actually the eggs that are harvested, and they are used primarily as fish food. The nearly 100 billion brine flies are also the main food supply to the millions of birds who use the lake and surrounding marshlands as part of their migratory pattern.

The Great Salt Lake has a tremendous effect on the weather for the region. Since the lake never freezes due to the salt content, cold fronts passing over collect an abundance of water and dump it into the valley and mountains to the east of the lake. During the summer months, cooler air will also settle over the warmer water. You can watch the storm clouds develop and drift eastward, with spectacular thunderstorms lighting up the valley. The lake is attributed to 10 percent of the average precipitation for Salt Lake City.

The **Saltair** has been rebuilt several times over the years due to devastating fires and floods. Today it is mainly used for concerts, and it's a great place to take a photograph of your day. For the latest concert information, you can visit their website, www.thesaltair.com. The history here is incredible, and you can almost feel the colorful times of yore call out as you walk the shore past this historic building. Just like countless visitors from US presidents to Gandhi, you'll find that this was and still is the place to be.

Bonneville Salt Flats. Approximately 85 miles west of Salt Lake City on I-80; (801) 977-4300; www.saltflats.com. We wonder if this was the place where they coined the phrase "fast cars and hot women." Now before you wonder what we are getting at, "hot" can also apply to the men in this hot, high, dry desert. In the summer the temperatures will exceed 100 degrees Fahrenheit. As for fast cars, we mean really fast cars. The Bonneville Salt Flats is world renowned for its land speed records. Imagine traveling over 600 miles per hour—or the next time you are flying in an airplane, ask if you can hang your head out the window and you will experience the thrill of the racers here at the salt flats. This unique natural feature of Utah stretches over 30,000 acres. This is a place designed for speed because it is so flat it is said you can see the curvature of the planet.

Nothing, not even the simplest form of life, can survive here. Some might argue that fact when they pass the "Metaphor: The Tree of Utah." This 87-foot oddity is the creation of Swedish artist Karl Momen, who after he was done, donated the work to the State of Utah in 1986. His goal was to provide a spot of bright color and a little beauty in this vast, barren landscape. Keep in mind that there are no facilities at the salt flats, so it is a bring-your-own-everything venue.

where to shop

Saltair Gift Shop. 12408 Saltair, Magna; (801) 250-4388; www.thesaltair.com. Open 7 days a week from 9 a.m. to 6 p.m. This is a great place to get souvenirs and famous salt-water taffy.

where to eat

Saltair Gift Shop. 12408 Saltair, Magna; (801) 250-4388; www.thesaltair.com. Open 7 days a week from 9 a.m. to 6 p.m. Stop and stock up on an assortment of sandwiches, drinks, candy, and ice cream before heading to the salt flats. $

day trip 02

west

shake, rattle & roll:
west wendover (nevada), blue lake

West Wendover is a little place to, well, indulge a bit; and it's just over the Utah state line to keep it all legal. Literally out in the middle of nowhere, lights appear in the desert, illuminating a small oasis to offer respite. West Wendover Will, the 50-foot neon cowboy, welcomes you to the lively town of West Wendover (though now he's been moved to the city center next to the City Hall). You can imagine this being what Las Vegas looked and felt like in the early days. Yes, this is the place to throw down the dice and catch some incredible, top-notch acts in the showroom, but West Wendover has a lot more to offer than just being a mini-Vegas.

getting there

From Salt Lake City, travel due west on I-80 for 120 miles and exit just as you pass over the Utah-Nevada border at exit 410.

where to go

West Wendover Tourism and Convention Bureau. 735 Wendover Blvd., West Wendover, NV; (775) 664-3138 or (866) 299-2989.

West Wendover Casinos and Resorts. Here you will find high-end casinos without the high-end price. Think of Las Vegas in the '60s or maybe '70s, when your dollar went much further, other than at the roulette table. The **Peppermill, Rainbow, Red Garter, Montego**

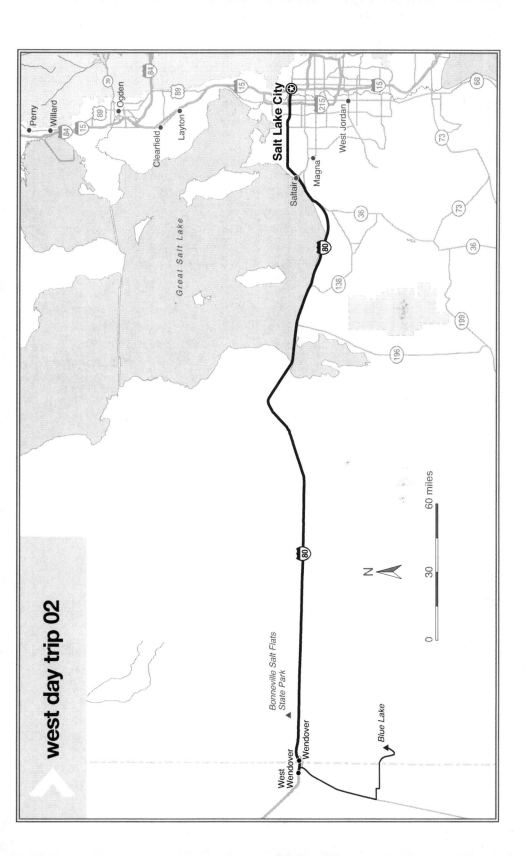

west day trip 02

Bay, and **Wendover Nugget** are the big-name casinos. Try your luck on a table or at the seat of a "one-armed bandit." Maybe unwind and relax at one of the European-type spas, or play a round of golf. Here the course is truly an oasis, intertwining the rugged natural desert as hazards and contrast to the green fairways. The entertainment is first class, bringing in some of the biggest stars in the entertainment industry, but with prices much lower than you'll find on the Vegas Strip. Many of the shows sell out early, so check the casino websites before you show up. Visit www.wendoverfun.com for more information.

Take advantage of the low rates in West Wendover and make it an extended stay as a base camp for exploring the other incredible attractions. Mountain biking, ATVing, and horseback riding are among the most popular. From the top of Three Mile Mountain, you can actually see the curvature of the earth.

Historic Wendover Airfield Museum. 345 S Airport Apron, Wendover, UT. Open daily from 8 a.m. to 6:30 p.m., 7 days a week. (To be admitted, you must arrive at least 1 hour before closing.) With little fanfare, Wendover played an important role in World War II. This is where training took place for the heavy bomber groups as they prepared for deployment overseas. It is also where history was made as the 509th Composite Group—the *Enola Gay* and *Bockscar*—trained before their deployment, carrying the atomic bombs to Japan. See and feel a part of history in your self-guided tour. The history doesn't end with World War II, either. This is also the site where many Hollywood pictures were filmed: *Hulk, The Core, Independence Day, Mulholland Falls, Con Air, Wind,* and *Philadelphia Experiment.*

Either make another day trip or plan your day trip around the annual Wendover Wings and Wheels Air Show. Held in Sept, it combines vintage cars with the roar of jets above. To get to the museum from Wendover Boulevard in Nevada, turn south on US 93; then take a left on Airport Way, cross the border into Utah, and turn right on 2nd Street. If you are coming from Salt Lake, take exit 1 on the Utah side and turn left on 1st Street. 1st Street will turn into 2nd Street, which will lead you to the airfield.

blue lake

About 20 miles south of Wendover, back on the Utah side, is a unique large body of water. In the middle of the wilderness is a place where you can swim and snorkel year-round. This warm spring-fed lake is known for excellent visibility and friendly fish. Warm may be an understatement and may depend on how deep you go. The deeper you venture, the hotter it gets, reaching 83 degrees near the bottom. Enjoy the warm water, and bring your scuba gear if you have some, as this is a popular site with depths to 55 feet. If you don't have scuba gear, bring your snorkel equipment and see the variety of fish. The bluegills love to be fed by hand. This is a more rustic location, so there are no facilities. Bring lots of sunscreen and bug repellent.

getting there

Take I-80 west to West Wendover and take the second Wendover exit (410). Turn left and then left again onto Wendover Boulevard. Drive 1 block and turn right on US 93. Follow south towards Ely and watch for the BLUE LAKE sign about 15 miles later. Turn left on the dirt road and head east 7 miles. You will cross the Utah border and you will be at Blue Lake.

where to eat

Coco Palms. 680 Wendover Blvd., West Wendover, NV; (775) 664-2255. Open 24 hours daily. Best known for their breakfasts, the Coco Palms is located in the Peppermill Casino. They seem to be a step above the other casinos for food, with great menus for lunch and dinner, too. $$

Salt Flats Cafe. 1 N. Bonneville Speedway Rd., Wendover, UT; (435) 665-7550. Open every day 9 a.m. to 9 p.m., this is the place where the locals eat. They have wonderful Mexican food and a low-key atmosphere. If you go during Bonneville race times, prepare to wait, as this is where everyone goes. If you are into racing, you will love all the pictures on the wall. The tacos are a local favorite as well as the breakfast. $

The Steakhouse. 1045 Wendover Blvd., West Wendover, NV; (800) 537-0207, ext. 36504. Located in the Rainbow Casino, it is known as the best steak house in town. It is the kind of place that when you eat there, you forget you are in the middle of the desert. While reservations are not required, it is best to make them, especially on the weekend. The Steakhouse is open every day except Mon and Tues. $$$

northwest

day trip 01

northwest

where the buffalo roam:
davis county

Life has so many adventures to take pleasure in that when you can find those few that are not only accessible but also affordable, that is when the adventure becomes a delight. Davis County offers many accessible and affordable delights, and they are only minutes apart. Here you are close to hiking, world-class downhill ski slopes, golf, and much more. In this remarkable area you can ski in the morning and tee off in the afternoon.

getting there

Driving north from Salt Lake City on I-15, take exit 332 off I-15; then drive west on Antelope Drive (UT 108 and 127) for 7 miles to the park entrance.

where to go

Antelope Island. 4528 W. 1700 South, Syracuse; (801) 773-2941; www.stateparks.utah .gov/parks/antelope-island. Antelope Island is aptly named because you will see herds of beautiful rust and white pronghorn antelope. But that is not all you will find on this island day trip. If you want to know where the buffalo roam, you need go no farther than the short drive to the largest island in the Great Salt Lake. Antelope Island State Park is home to a roaming herd of about 500 bison. There is a who's who of wild big game, as the island is also home to mule deer, coyote, bighorn sheep, and other large and small animals. The wildlife thrives on this island of grassland, wetland, and miles and miles of shoreline, even though it is surrounded by water that is five times saltier than the ocean.

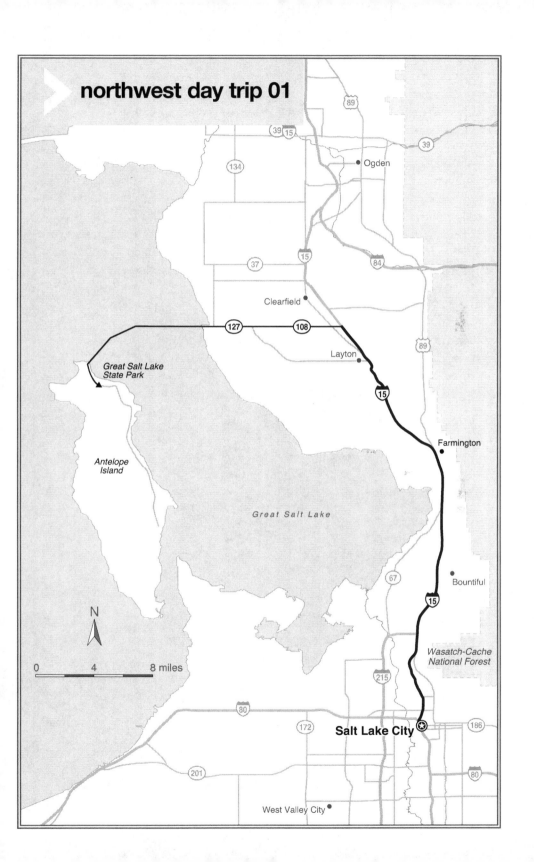

The rangelands have the most remarkable views overlooking the lake, plus unbeliev-able backcountry trails that are open for mountain camping, biking, hiking, cross-country skiing, and horseback riding.

A quick drive across the causeway, the narrow road that runs from the mainland to the island, and you will feel as though you are on the plains of Wyoming. Transported from the hectic and busy city life, you enter into the sanctuary of this lovely island surrounded by the desert sea, and bask in the sun while enjoying the beauties of the wild.

There are incredible white-sand beaches for playing, picnicking, and sunbathing. A charming sailboat marina at the south end of the Great Salt Lake lets boaters choose an alternative route to the island. In addition to the marina, there are primitive camping areas.

Antelope Island's elevation is 4,200 feet at the shore and 6,596 feet at the highest point, Frary Peak. With a total of 28,022 acres and measuring 15 miles long and 7 miles wide at its widest point, the island is a natural gem in the midst of city life.

The cost for a day visit is $9 per vehicle or $3 per cyclist or pedestrian. Park hours vary greatly, so plan ahead: July to mid-Sept from 7 a.m. to 10 p.m.; mid-Sept to Oct 1 from 7 a.m. to 8 p.m.; Oct 2 to mid-Nov from 7 a.m. to 7 p.m.; mid-Nov to Feb from 7 a.m. to 5 p.m.; Mar 1 to May 1 from 7 a.m. to 8 p.m.; May 2 to July from 7 a.m. to 9 p.m.

- **Visitor center and Fielding Garr Ranch House.** There are 2 very unique attributes about the house. First, it is the oldest continually inhabited Anglo home in the state of Utah; second, it is the oldest Anglo-built house in Utah still on its original foundation. Open Apr 15 to Sept 14 from 9 a.m. to 6 p.m. and Sept 15 to Apr 14 from 9 a.m. to 5 p.m. Closed Thanksgiving and Christmas.

- **Camping.** Bridger Bay Campground is $13 a night. White Rock Bay Group camp-grounds charge $3 per person (25 person minimum and 150 maximum). Bridger Bay also has freshwater showers so you can spray off that salty water after taking a dip or playing on the beach.

- **Horseback riding.** (801) 774-8200; call at least 48 hours beforehand. The cost begins at around $50 per hour, and riders must be at least 6 years of age.

- **Kayak and canoe rentals.** If you don't own a kayak or canoe, don't worry. The great people at South Davis Rental in North Salt Lake will set you up for $20 a day; (801) 299-0880. If you're coming from the north, it might be easier to stop at the Weber State Outdoor Program. They can rent you all the equipment you need; (801) 626-6373.

- **Bicycle rentals.** Bountiful Bicycle Center in North Salt Lake/Bountiful will rent out bikes for about $50 a day; they also have a rack that attaches to your trailer hitch for rent. (801) 295-6711.

There are also many scheduled activities that are offered throughout the year:

- **Art gallery exhibit.** For more information call (801) 725-9263.

farmington bay waterfowl management area

Located south and west of Farmington, on the eastern edge of the Great Salt Lake. This is nothing like the Alfred Hitchcock film The Birds—*you will go away in awe not horror! With over 200 species of birds, you can imagine the varieties that can be seen, especially during the migrating seasons. You could see hundreds of thousands of waterbirds, songbirds, and raptors, thankfully not from Jurassic Park!*

To get a closer look at the birds and animals, you can use spotting scopes and binoculars; photographers will need a telephoto lens. Some of the best viewing can be done from your car, while you are driving slowly along the back roads.

Spring and fall are the ideal times to view the migrating birds, from Mar to May or Aug to Oct. There are many birds that choose to "keep house" here year-round. Early morning or late evening hours are the best for finding the birds and animals most active. 1325 W. Glover Lane, Farmington (925 South); open daily (the main entrance) from 8 a.m. to 5 p.m.; the other entrance hours vary by season.

- **Children's Roundup.** This event gets the kids involved with the annual bison roundup.

- **Bison Roundup.** Put on your cowboy hat and boots and join in the fun! You can watch the volunteer cowboys and cowgirls bring in the herd.

- **Bison Auction.** To maintain a healthy herd number, the park will annually auction off over 100 bison.

- **Bison health check.** Come watch the volunteers and staff begin a history on the health of each newborn calf and check the health of the remaining bison.

- ***Our Inland Sea: Exploring the Great Salt Lake.*** Watch the 45-minute documentary about the Great Salt Lake at the visitor center.

where to eat

Island Buffalo Grill. Located on Antelope Island; (801) 528-8080 or (801) 499-9291. How venturesome are you? Can you play with the bison in the morning and then order a buffalo burger or buffalo bratwurst for lunch? They serve some of the best buffalo burgers, not to mention the other scrumptious food, at the Island Buffalo Grill. This will truly be an experience for the whole family. The best part of traveling is the opportunity to try new and exotic foods. Here's your chance to try something new yet, oh, so good—and you don't have to travel thousands of miles to get there. Open Mon to Sun from 11 a.m. to 6 p.m. $

day trip 02

northwest

"driving the last spike"
promontory

"All aboard!" Take a drive to one of the most historical places in Utah. If you are a railroad buff or even a history lover, Promontory has to be high on your to-do list in Utah. Back when rail was king, this place was the crown jewel—or at least the "golden spike." What began as a race between two railroads from two major cities, Omaha in the east and Sacramento in the west, ended in what was then the tent town of Promontory. What started out as the United States' first Transcontinental Railroad turned out to provide not only history, but innovation as well. On May 10, 1869, the Union Pacific railroad tracks connected with those of the Central Pacific, creating the first continuous railroad spanning the nation. As you walk around this historic site, you can imagine the excitement of the thousands who gathered. It was now possible to travel safely from New York to California by rail. What would have taken months to traverse on horseback or stagecoach just days before would now take mere days by rail.

This railroad was considered by many to be the greatest engineering achievement of the 19th century. From its humble yet significant rail beginnings, Promontory continues to generate engineering achievements at its ATK Thiokol plant, a premier aerospace and defense company. We wonder what those standing here in 1869 would think to hear the roar of a solid rocket engine being tested so close to this historic place. The same rocket booster that has been used to take men into the new frontier of space was built right near the site of the old frontier of the Wild West.

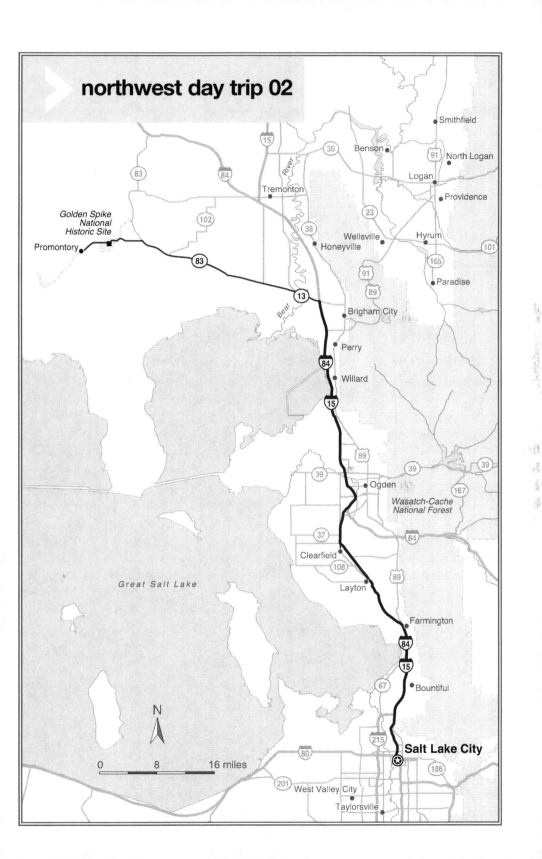

getting there

From Salt Lake City, travel north on I-15 for 58 miles. Take exit 365 and merge onto SR 13/ Promontory Road. Take a slight left at SR 83 North and travel 17.5 miles. Turn left on 7200 North and continue 2 miles until you reach a Y. Turn right onto 18400 West for 2 miles. The Golden Spike will be on your left. Continue on 7200 North and take a left at 22000 West to Promontory.

where to go

ATK Rocket Garden. Located on SR 83 in Promontory, just 26 miles northwest of Brigham City on SR 83, and east of the Golden Spike National Historic Site. The rocket garden in front of the Thiokol Corporation's manufacturing facility displays a space shuttle rocket booster, a Patriot missile, and several other rockets and rocket motors. Open and free to the public, this display of space hardware is a great visual presentation on the history of aerospace exploration.

Golden Spike National Historic Site. Located 32 miles west of Brigham City via SR 13 and SR 83; (435) 471-2209; www.nps.gov/gosp. What some dubbed "the Mountain Wedding" really started off as more of a shotgun wedding. Knowing the importance of the completion of a single railroad line between the eastern and western United States, Congress forced the two competing railroads into a marriage of national convenience. The Golden Spike National Historic Site offers 5 entertaining and informative films, shown regularly at the visitor center. During the winter months the locomotives are kept in the Engine House for repairs and maintenance. Engine House tours are usually available from 10 a.m. to 4 p.m., but tour availability may be subject to change, so call (435) 471-2209, ext. 29 to check schedules. While at the park, enjoy a 1½-mile round-trip walking trail. The Big Fill Loop Trail allows you to walk through cuts and over fills; here you will see drill marks where workers blasted rock away.

Witness the reenactment ceremony at the same location where the original ceremony took place. The ceremony is held each Sat and on holidays between May and Oct at 11 a.m. and 1 p.m. Entrance fees include a vehicle fee of $7 in the summer, $5 in the winter. The fee is good for all persons riding in a private, noncommercial vehicle. If you are entering by bicycle or motorcycle, the fee is only $4 in the summer, $3 in the winter. Fee-free days are May 10 (the anniversary of the completion of the Transcontinental Railroad) and Aug 14 (Railroader's Festival).

where to shop

Golden Spike National Historic Site Visitor Center. Situated 32 miles west of Brigham City via SR 13 and SR 83, the visitor center can be contacted at (435) 471-2209, ext. 29. The visitor center hours are 9 a.m. to 5 p.m. daily; closed New Year's, Thanksgiving, and Christmas. Outside attractions are open during daylight hours. Here you can pick up your own reminder of this significant place in time and history.

appendix a:
festivals & celebrations

january

Utah Winter Games, statewide. Athletes of all ages and abilities can participate in winter sports such as skiing, skating, and luging. (435) 658-4208; www.utahwintergames.org.

Sundance Film Festival, Park City. Internationally celebrated film festival, founded in 1984 by Robert Redford, convening every Jan to show independent films. www.sundance.org/festival.

Hof Winterfest German Festival, Ogden. Authentic German food and Bavarian music are enjoyed by over 3,500 people annually during the 2-day event. (800) 399-8227.

St. George Winter Bird Festival, St. George. Come learn and explore many birding areas in southwest Utah. Presentations, field trips, and workshops available for experienced and beginners alike. (435) 634-5800; www.sgcity.org/birdfestival.

february

Bryce Canyon Winter Fest, Bryce Canyon City. Ruby's Inn hosts this 3-day event offering snow activities, tours, clinics, food, music, and more. Ruby's Inn, 26 S. Main St.; (866) 866-6616.

march

Delta Snow Goose Festival, Delta. At the second largest wildlife festival in Utah there are thousands of snow geese upon the water and in the air. http://deltagoosefestival.info/festival.

St. Patrick's Day Parade, Salt Lake City. This 7-block parade features all things green and Irish with floats, bands, and cars. Afterward, keep celebrating during the Siamsa, the post-parade party. (801) 463-7849.

april

St. George Art Festival, St. George. For 30 years this festival has picked only 110 artists to showcase, from local artists to those throughout the western US. www.sgcity.org/artfestival.

Canyonlands Film Festival, Moab. Founded in 1995, this festival features video art and independent films from all over the world. http://moab-utah.com/film/video/festival.html.

Arch Canyon Jeep Jamboree, Blanding. This event takes place in one of the most beautiful places in the Canyonlands, the home of the "Ancient Ones"; Anasazi Indians have been in this area for thousands of years. The off-road weekend adventure is for those wanting to do trail drives with Jeep 4x4s. (530) 333-4777; www.jeepjamboreeusa.com.

may

Scandinavian Heritage Festival, Ephraim. Festival grounds on the north side of Snow College come alive with storytelling, dancing, entertainment, costumes, tours, and craft and food booths. (435) 835-4241.

Great Salt Lake Bird Fest, Farmington. Birders will enjoy this festival with its many field trips, workshops, presentations, and fun for kids. www.greatsaltlakebirdfest.com.

Old Ephraim's Mountain Man Rendezvous, Hyrum. This event re-creates the adventure of time gone by. Play kids' games and see primitive shooting and archery, Dutch oven cooking, and traders. (435) 245-3778.

San Raphael Swell Spring Mountain Bike Fest, Huntington. Beginners and expert bike enthusiasts will find a perfect ride by the beautiful San Raphael Swell. Campfires, stories, and the Dutch oven cookouts give many opportunities to connect with others. (435) 653-2500.

june

Utah Summer Games (Extreme Sports Weekend), Cedar City. Aspiring athletes can challenge themselves in 40 different "Olympic" sports during this weekend. Almost 10,000 Utahan's participate (athletes must be Utah residents) in this annual event started in 1986. (435) 865-8421; www.utahsummergames.org.

Tuacahn, Ivins. Thousands come to visit the plays at the beautiful 1,920-seat Tuacahn amphitheater, set in the mouth of Padre Canyon below 1,500-foot red sandstone cliffs. The amphitheater presents professional musical productions as part of the "Broadway in the Desert" series and gives high school students the opportunity to participate in an 8-week summer camp. Regular season June through Oct. (800) 746-9882; http://tuacahn.org.

Summerfest Arts Faire, Logan. Come visit Logan's Historic Downtown Tabernacle Square, where more than 130 artists are featured every year. There is the children's art yard, good food, entertainment, and concerts every evening. (435) 213-3858; www.logan summerfest.com.

Mormon Miracle Pageant, Manti. This Mormon historical drama is held under the stars at the foot of the Manti Temple. (866) 961-9040; http://mormonmiracle.org.

Utah Arts Fest, Salt Lake City. This downtown 4-day festival brings more than 80,000 visitors and features fine arts, live performances, theater, film, and food. (801) 322-2428; www.uaf.org.

Shakespeare Festival summer season, Cedar City. In addition to the 6 plays offered, the festival features nightly Greenshows with music, tales, and songs on the outdoor stages. Literary seminars, play discussions, backstage tours and orientations are also available. (800) PLAYTIX; www.bard.org.

july

Days of '47 (Utah Pioneer Day celebrations), statewide. On July 24, 1847, pioneers made a trek into Utah Territory. This is celebrated during the Days of '47, with a parade, rodeo, and royalty pageant. (801) 250-3890; www.daysof47.com.

Payson Scottish Festival, Payson. As the only free Scottish festival in the western US, this community sponsored event is for all. Come share in Scottish traditions with traditional food, bagpipes, Highland athletic competitions, a parade, and activities for children. www .paysonscottishfestival.org.

Boulder Heritage Festival, Boulder. Boulder's diverse and rich history is celebrated during this festival. From the ancient Anasazis, to the pioneer settlers, to our present community, we wish to educate and celebrate our history. Come enjoy food, music, and entertainment. (435) 335-7550.

august

Bear Lake Raspberry Days, Garden City. During this raspberry harvest festival, thousands come to taste the delicious crop. The festival includes a parade, a rodeo, craft booths, and fireworks. (800) 448-BEAR; www.bearlake.org/raspdays.html.

Park City Jazz Festival, Park City. Come join the nonstop entertainment, sit on the gently sloping hill of the Deer Valley Resort ski runs, and enjoy the beautiful view and "Jazz with Altitude." The festival also features a village of vendors, a beer garden, and a live video board broadcast of performances. (435) 649-1000; www.parkcityjazz.org.

Railroaders Festival, Promontory (Golden Spike National Historic Site). This festival draws history and railroad enthusiasts from around the country. Tour the 2 fully functional locomotive replicas, take handcar rides, and enjoy an 1860s fashion show, food, games, and entertainment. (435) 471-2209, ext. 29.

Belly Dance Festival, Snowbird. This is the largest gathering of belly-dancing fans, with over 15,000 visitors and 400 performers. Shows are free, and seminars with featured artists are available for a fee. (801) 486-7780; www.aros.net/~kismet.

Rockport Dam Jam, Rockport State Park. Bluegrass and camping collide during this festival, located at Rockport's Old Church campground area. Come listen, jam, or dance along. Potluck dinner nightly. (435) 336-2241.

september

Oktoberfest, Snowbird. The history of Oktoberfest started in 1810 to celebrate the autumn marriage of King Ludwig. It was dedicated to celebrate the fall harvest and beer, which was Munich's most famous product. Snowbird's Oktoberfest has been celebrating for 38 years, attracting over 50,000 visitors. Food, vendors, entertainment, and fun for all ages. www .snowbird.com.

Peach Days, Brigham City. Starting in 1904 as a day off from the harvest, this is said to be the second oldest harvest festival in the country. Window displays, fruit displays, parade, pageants, and entertainment. (435) 723-3931.

Shakespeare Festival fall season, Cedar City. The fall schedule offers 3 different plays in the Randall L. Jones Theatre. Also available are literary seminars, actor's seminars, pro seminars, backstage tours, and play orientations. (800) PLAYTIX; www.bard.org.

Green River Melon Days, Green River. Celebrate the end of the melon season with arts and crafts, craft boutiques, and games. www.greenriverutah.com/melondays.html.

Old Capital Arts and Living History Festival, Fillmore. This 2-day event takes place at the Territorial Statehouse Park, with mountain-man demonstrations, live entertainment, and fine art. (435) 743-5316.

Fall Harvest Festival, Logan. Celebrate the harvest season at the American West Heritage Center with a corn maze, train rides, pony rides, and a kids' pirate hay fort. www.awhc.org.

Camp Floyd Days, Camp Floyd/Stagecoach Inn State Park and Museum. Participate in reenactments performed by soldiers of Johnston's Army, storytelling, stagecoach rides, and a camp experience. The event also features 1861 period games, firearm and cannon demonstrations, marches, drills, and photos in uniform. (801) 768-8932.

Swiss Days, Midway. Swiss Days has become a major event in the beautiful high mountain town of Midway. A wide variety of handmade items, fine art, antiques, and fine Swiss food are available. www.midwayswissdays.com.

Moab Music Festival, Moab. This festival is called "music in concert with the landscape" because it brings musicians to play in the stunning red-rock venues. Travel down the Colorado River in a jet boat to the unique grotto concerts. (435) 259-7003; www.moabmusic fest.org.

Ogden Nature Center Wildlands Bash, Ogden. This event is meant to bring together people with nature and create a better appreciation of the environment. Come enjoy jazzy music, a gourmet dinner, and auction. Call (801) 621-7595 for reservations.

Payson's Onion Days, Payson. This community event has a carnival, boutique, and entertainment. (801) 465-6031.

Greek Festival, Salt Lake City. Share in the "Greek Spirit of Life" during the Greek fest, with music, food, and more. www.saltlakegreekfestival.com.

Antelope Island Balloon and Kite Fest, Antelope Island State Park. Watch hot-air balloons as they go over the park and the Great Salt Lake. Bring your own kite to fly and enjoy the live music, food, crafts, and games. www.antelopeballoons.com.

october

Ghosts of Camp Floyd, Camp Floyd/Stagecoach Inn State Park and Museum. Do you want to learn ghost-hunting techniques? Bring your recorders and cameras to try to capture paranormal finds. Hear previous recordings and view photos and other evidence from historical Camp Floyd. (801) 768-8932.

World Land Speed Finals, Bonneville Salt Flats, Wendover. Thousands travel to this 7-day event at the "fastest place on earth" to view vehicles racing at high speeds. www.landracing .com.

The Huntsman World Senior Games, St. George. This international competition is available for athletes 50 and older. Health screenings are also provided to promote good health and physical fitness as a way of daily life. (800) 562-1268.

november

Iron Mission Days, Cedar City. Celebrate Cedar City's birthday and pioneer heritage. Family handcart pulls, pioneer craft demonstrations, and tours of the historic cemetery. (435) 586-9390.

Moab Folk Festival, Moab. This music festival features musicians and bands at 3 venues throughout the city. www.moabfolkfestival.com.

december

American Children's Christmas Festival, Cedar City. Enjoy bedtime stories, musical and dance productions, a festival of trees, Santa Land, and fireworks at Cedar City Heritage Center. (435) 865-5107; www.christmas-festival.org.

Christmas in the Canyon and Live Nativity, Ivins. As a way of saying "thank you" to the community, Tuacahn's Christmas in the Canyon seeks to celebrate the true meaning of Christmas. A Live Nativity is held in the amphitheater at 7 and 8 p.m. nightly. Visitors can see lights and hear wonderful Christmas music on the Tuachan Plaza. (800) 746-9882; www.tuacahn.org.

Christmas at the Homestead, Cedar City. Activities at the Frontier Homestead State Park and Museum include a warm fire, quilt and paper-chain making, a pioneer Christmas story, popcorn stringing, and a visit with Santa. (435) 586-9290.

appendix b: spas

bountiful

Garden Day Spa and Salon. 299 N. 200 West; (801) 294-4247; www.gardendayspaand salon.com. Whether you are choosing to be pampered or you have an exciting occasion, such as a wedding, Garden Day Spa can help you feel relaxed and refreshed. Open Mon from 11 a.m. to 7 p.m., Tues to Fri 9 a.m. to 8 p.m., and Sat 9 a.m. to 5 p.m.; closed on Sun.

brian head

Cedar Breaks Day Spa. Located in the Cedar Breaks Lodge, 223 Hunter Ridge Rd.; (435) 677-4225; www.cedarbreakslodge.com. The tranquility of Brian Head will have guests feeling rejuvenated and relaxed. Holistic services include hot-stone therapies, aromatherapy, and salt scrubs. The Swedish massage will ease your sore muscles and the pearl skin polish will enliven the senses, and these are just two of their distinctive services. Your experience at Brian Head can be made even more complete with special in-room treatment options.

The Red Leaf Spa. The Grand Lodge at Brian Head, 314 Hunter Ridge Dr.; (435) 677-9000, ext. 108; www.grandlodgebrianhead.com/spa. After a day on the mountain, take some time to indulge and relax at the Red Leaf Spa. With its earthy and serene atmosphere, guests will feel like they have entered another world. Relaxation will be inevitable. All services include complimentary use of the sauna, hot tub, steam room, pool, and fitness center. Several signature services are provided, including the Mountain Man Massage. This includes aromatherapy and a special sportsman massage designed especially for men.

heber city

Retreat Day Spa. Daniels Summit Pass, US 40; Located in the Daniels Summit Lodge; (435) 538-2300; www.danielssummit.com. Trained massage therapists use Swedish techniques to work out even the most stubborn knots. Body wraps and many other specialized treatments are also available. There are also Retreat Spa lodging packages available for an exclusive weekend getaway.

moab

Sorrel River Ranch and Spa. Mile 17, UT 128; (877) 359-2715; www.sorrelriver.com. A large array of massage therapy and spa services are available at this intimate and inviting spa. This allows personnel to offer a very focused and individualized set of services to relax guests. Guests can also receive holistic treatments.

midway

Homestead Resort Spa. Homestead Resort; 700 N. Homestead Dr.; (866) 931-3097; www.homesteadresort.com/spa. Prior to all treatments, guests have the opportunity to receive a complimentary service, such as a foot bath. Complimentary treatments are available in the outdoor Mineral Water Soaking Tub. (For these services you must arrive early.) Their Elemental Nature treatment is one of their most popular. Enjoy your treatments within the natural surroundings and professional atmosphere that will leave you feeling renewed. Hours of operation are seasonal; call for details.

The Spa at Zermatt. 784 W. Resort Dr.; (435) 709-9596; www.zermattresort.com. Located in Heber Valley, Zermatt is inspired by the traditional baths and spas in Europe. During you visit you can enjoy the use of all the facilities, which include a fitness center, dry sauna, aromatherapy steam grotto, waterfall hot tub, indoor and outdoor swimming pools, and more. The Spa at Zermatt provides treatments, education, holistic classes, and cardiovascular and weight training equipment to help give balance and a healthier lifestyle. Each treatment will promote a deep level of relaxations, with a staff that plays particular attention to detail. Open Sun through Thurs 10 a.m. to 6 p.m. and Fri through Sat 9 a.m. to 9 p.m.

park city

Amatsu Spa at the Sky Lodge. The Sky Lodge, 201 Heber Ave. at Main St.; (888) 876-2525; www.theskylodge.com. According to the Sky Lodge, the Amatsu Spa will give you "an infused, organic, Zen-influenced experience." The breathing treatment (from Japan) will begin with their Ofuro soak, which is a cleansing purification, and you'll then be awakened with a mandarin scrub followed by an Oolong tea shea-butter quench wrap; then there's a final hydrating Earth shower. Other massages include: Amatsu-Ni (couples massage), Bamboo-Koi, Tasan Mother, Amatsu therapeutic, and Amatsu signature massage. Leave feeling pampered by these and all their tantalizing and relaxing offerings. Open daily, but you must make advanced reservations.

The Canyons Grand Summit Hotel Health Club and Spa. The Canyon Resort, 400 Canyons Resort Dr.; (435) 615-8035; www.thecanyons.com. Commitment to helping guests obtain relief from stress, aches, and daily worries is the focus of this spa. They offer many different services, including body and couples therapy; facial, hand, and toes therapy; wedding packages; massage therapy; and more. Being pampered by several different therapies will help you leave with a smile on your face. Open daily from 9 a.m. to 9 p.m. The Health Club is open 24 hours a day, 7 days a week.

Golden Door Waldorf Astoria Park City. Waldorf Astoria Park City, 2100 West Frostwood Blvd.; (866) 279-0843; www.goldendoor.com/parkcity. Golden Door Spa has captured the spirit of the ancient honjin inns of Japan by providing proven traditional and modern techniques: stone massage, shirodhara, lymphatic massage, acupuncture, and much more. Begin the quest to make the change to soothe your body and refresh your soul.

Serenity Spa by Westgate. Westgate Park City Resort, 3000 Canyons Resorts Dr.; (435) 655-2266; www.wgparkcity.com. The name truly reflects the feeling you will have by experiencing the ultimate relaxation in their luxury spa. They feature a full menu of the best therapeutic treatments, exercise faculties, and amenities that will have you feeling rejuvenated and refreshed. If you are looking for a place to de-stress and unwind, the Serenity Spa will give you an unforgettable experience.

The Spa at Hotel Park City. Hotel Park City, 2001 Park Ave.; (435) 940-5080; www
.hotelparkcity.com. Inspired by the natural surroundings of Utah's mountain wilderness and forests, this spa offers herbal-infused steam rooms, dry saunas, meditation rooms, whirlpools, a health club, a full hair salon, and much more. Among their plethora of massages, they offer a couples massage and soak in a suite designed for 2, focus massage, reflexology massage, aromatherapy massage, nurturing mother, and therapeutic deep-tissue massage. Call to make a reservation.

The Spa at Stein Eriksen Lodge. The Eriksen Lodge, 7700 Stein Way; (435) 645-6475; www.steinlodge.com/spa. Reawaken your spirit by visiting their luxurious Norwegian spa, which will give you ample space to experience a balance of tranquility and rejuvenation. All of their 16 treatment rooms include access to a sauna, steam room, and a hot and cold plunge. They even feature 2 magnificent treatment rooms for couples, which include private showers, tubs, and a shared private relaxation suite with a fireplace. Call to make a reservation.

solitude

The Spa at Solitude. 12000 Big Cottonwood Canyon; (801) 535-4137; www.skisolitude
.com/village/spa_solitude.php. Located in the Inn at Solitude, the spa provides some of the most relaxing treatments (even in-room massages). After a day of adventure, unwind with a therapeutic body treatment, a deep-tissue massage, or one of their signature facial massages. If you are feeling fully indulgent, they offer several spa packages to choose from, plus many other services: hydros, facials, steam sauna, yoga, and the option to sit in the hot tub or pool as you enjoy the view of the beautiful Wasatch Mountains. Open daily from 9 a.m. to 8 p.m.

snowbird

The Cliff Spa at Snowbird. Snowbird Resort, The Cliff Lodge, Level 9, UT 210, Little Cottonwood Canyon; (801) 933-2225, ext. 5900; www.snowbird.com. For over 20 years the Cliff Spa has provided a tranquil and invigorating place of retreat. Here are just of a few treatments that they offer: reflexology, Thai yoga massage, high-altitude relief, superior stone therapy, cranial sacred therapy, etc. Their goal is to "provide an experience of solitude and reflection leaving you refreshed and inspired." Call for reservations.

spring city

Nature Spa at Wind Walker Guest Ranch. Wind Walker Guest Ranch; 11550 Pigeon Hollow Rd.; (435) 462-0282; www.windwalker.org. You will find all things in nature used to create the perfect balance at the Wind Walker Guest Ranch: Tai Chi, guided meditations, sweat lodges, spirituality exploration, massage, energy balancing, stone therapy, ear coning, facials and pedicures, chakra alignment, touch for health, light body anatomy, stress-release training, Native American medicine wheels, and much more.

sundance

Spa at Sundance. Sundance Resort; 8841 North Alpine Loop Rd.; (801) 223-4270; www .sundanceresort-px.rtrk.com. The Spa at Sundance is inspired by the Sioux concept of *hocoka,* which means "a sacred environment for the restoration and healing of the spirit and body." In their alluring and eco-friendly treatment rooms, they blend Native American traditions, naturally pure products, and human contact to bring your body, mind, and spirit back into supreme balance. The spa states: "Our goal . . . is to unify by the Native American concept of the Four Winds. Here the four directions of the earth bond with the four seasons, the cycles of life, and our physical being, which brings clarity to our connection with the universe." Open during the summer from 9 a.m. to 8 p.m. and winter from 10 a.m. to 7 p.m.

wellsville

Sherwood Hills Resort Conference Center and Spa. Sherwood Hills Resort and Conference Center; 7877 S. US 89/91; (435) 245-5054; www.sherwoodhills.com. Experience one of the finest European-style spas in northern Utah. They offer an entire selection of rejuvenating spa services: neck and back massage, classic Swedish massage, deep-tissue massage, and aromatherapy massages. You can also experience treatments in a relaxing atmosphere with a variety of luxurious skin, scalp, manicure, and pedicure options.

index